Seven C's
of Marriage

Dr. Gbadebo, -
May you grow in
love !

Amy Bindas

Sailing the Seven C's of Marriage

*Having the Marriage
You've Always Wanted*

AMY BINDAS

TATE PUBLISHING
AND ENTERPRISES, LLC

Published by Tate Publishing & Enterprises, LLC
127 E. Trade Center Terrace | Mustang, Oklahoma 73064 USA
1.888.361.9473 | www.tatepublishing.com

Tate Publishing is committed to excellence in the publishing industry. The company reflects the philosophy established by the founders, based on Psalm 68:11,
"The Lord gave the word and great was the company of those who published it."

Published in the United States of America

ISBN: 978-1-62295-938-9
1. Religion / Christian Life / Love & Marriage
2. Family & Relationships / Marriage
12.11.06

Dedication

To my kind and loving husband, Steve, who affectionately refers to himself as "subject matter." We embarked on this marriage journey over seventeen years ago, and I have been so blessed by you ever since. Even though our journey encountered rough waters at the beginning, you stood by me, committed and unshaken, giving me the courage to examine myself and my role as a wife. My love for you grows deeper every day, and I can truly say that our marriage is everything I ever hoped it would be. Thank you so much for your love, strength, tenderness, and for often doing more than your fair share.

To Mark and Mollie, you have been mentors for Steve and I and countless others. Thank you for your transparency with each other and those around you. We have learned selflessness and unfailing love through your example. Mark, I appreciate your creative thinking and help with the Bible study. *Sailing the Seven Cs of Marriage* would not have come to fruition without you. Mollie, you are a fantastic wife and mother and a wonderful cheerleader. I am honored to have you in my corner.

And to my children, Evan and Jordan. You have been encouraging and supportive of my efforts to allow God to speak through me. If marriage is in your future, may this work help you establish the kind of marriage your father and I have. I have been praying for the wife God will provide you!

Acknowledgments

I wish to thank the following people for their help in making this work possible:

Mark Schuster for assisting with some of the research as well as cofacilitating our first Bible study together. You are a wonderful teacher and friend. God has used you to touch the lives of many.

Kristin Kreuser, whose valuable editing insights brought this work together effectively and clearly. I treasure your literary command, your honest opinions, but most of all, the friendship of you and your husband, Terry. We have discussed a lot of this material over the years, and you have always been a blessing to me.

To my supportive friends who have encouraged me on this new endeavor, Deb Neerdaels, Nancy Croy, and Shelly Hribernik. I hope I have offered you the gift of encouragement when you have needed it as you have offered me.

And finally, to the first Sailing the Seven Cs of Marriage Bible study group at Faith Lutheran Church. Thank you for your commitment to the process, your openness and honesty with each other, and the wonderful humor you brought each week. You provided awesome material.

Table of Contents

Introduction

When many of us first embark on the marriage journey, we are looking forward to an enticing adventure shared with the one we love. Picture a cruise to exotic locations where the calm breeze and warm sun make the anticipation of things to come cause joy to overflow in your heart. You board, bags packed, not looking back. You are excited, willing, and happy to sail off into the sunset.

Not long after leaving the harbor, you encounter a gentle little rock to the ship. Maybe your spouse said something that unknowingly hurt your feelings or you forgot to pack a crucial item that your spouse could, quite frankly, not care less about. Whatever the case may be, you see this initial rock in your "relational boat" as something that you will quickly pass through on your way to calmer seas. There are soon shared experiences that bring you closer as a couple, and the pictures you take on this initial leg of your sailing journey reflect two smiling mates still very much enamored with each other.

Eventually, more disagreements, thoughtless words, and hurt feelings come. The honeymoon part of the cruise has ended. You find yourself wondering, *Did I pick the wrong partner for my lifelong journey?* This may happen in the first year of marriage or the seventh or the twenty-first.

But for most of us, the reality is that it will happen! The beautiful ports of call on your itinerary begin to become routine and mundane, and some may begin to find their cabin confining or their travel mate in their way. We look back from the deck of our ship and see others on land that are still single, and we may think they have it made. We see them looking back at us, questioning whether or not to embark on such a journey where they will be tossed and turned.

Many couples find themselves slowly growing tired of the work that marriage involves. They wonder why their spouse doesn't appreciate them, doesn't acknowledge them, or doesn't ever seem to be on the same page. They grow increasingly frustrated with their spouse, their situation, and even themselves.

When looking at divorce rates among married couples today, the US Government Center for Disease Control and Prevention finds two similar studies. Jennifer Baker of the Forest Institute of Professional Psychology in Springfield, Missouri, cites that in America today, 50% of first marriages, 67% of second, and 74% of third marriages end in divorce, whereas the *Enrichment* journal on the divorce rate in America puts the statistics at 41% for first marriages, 60% for second, and 73% for third marriages respectively. Unfortunately, a 2008 study done by the Barna Group as cited in the *Christian Post* finds that Christians aren't doing much better than non-Christians. It found that the divorce rate in America is the same for Christians as for non-Christians at 33%—one-third of all marriages failing for both groups. Even though the statistics vary between the studies, we can say that one-third to one-half of all marriages end in divorce and that Christians aren't doing much better than non-Christians.

This is not taking into account the marriages that haven't legally ended but have ended emotionally. Often the journey has led the couple to dock at an unsightly port for repairs, and they have remained stuck there for years. How are we to be role models for God's great plan of marriage if we can't make it work? Nonbelievers look at believers in God's plan for marriage and make arguments for cohabitation and gay marriage as alternatives to an obviously flawed plan. Take heart. No matter how rocky or off course your marriage journey has been to this point, you can make the conscious effort to get back on course. We have to fight for our marriages and be courageous enough to enact God's plan the way it was intended. The key is that we have to work on ourselves instead of complaining that our spouse isn't doing what he or she should. It is easier to complain to our friends over coffee or a sporting event than it is to look in the mirror and decide what we need to fix. There is, however, a place where we can go for guidance and introspection. In God's word, the Bible, He has given us instructions to follow—if we would only listen. In doing so, I guarantee that you will not only be a bright light to others but to your spouse as well. You will have the marriage you've always wanted, and your journey in life will truly be the trip of a lifetime!

In order to enjoy the beautiful itinerary God has planned for those that marry, we will have to negotiate choppy waters and storms, but the end result will be a wonderful journey filled with love, laughter, and memories that will serve as an inspiration to others. Navigating the rough waters involves knowledge of the seven *C*s of marriage and how each of them is crucial to building a vessel strong enough to weather the storms. The seven *C*s include God's *command* to those that marry, the *commitment* that is needed, the art of *communication* with your spouse, making *couple time* a priority, having a plan for currency, making sure your marriage is *Christ-centered*, and finally, supporting each other in the larger *community*.

Having knowledge of and practicing the skills behind the seven *C*s will lead you to the realization that the marriage journey is not one that you should set out on so that you will be as happy as possible. It is a selfless journey in which you focus on making your spouse as happy as possible by following the course God has charted. He has given us His word to follow, and thus the Bible becomes the map we need to study and rely on to chart our course. Yes, storms will come. But you and your spouse can make it through together with the strength God gives you and the strength you give each other.

How to Approach This Book

My husband Steve and I joke (we call it joking now) that we have been married for seventeen years, "happily married" for eight. I found myself nine years into marriage with what everyone else said was a great guy, two beautiful children—Evan now age fifteen and Jordan now age twelve—but miserable. I saw myself growing increasingly frustrated and bitter. The honeymoon cruise—yes, we took a honeymoon cruise to exotic Caribbean locations—had turned into a day-to-day aimless journey breeding anger and resentment. I wondered why he didn't love me the way I yearned to be loved, and I became angry at the cold and heartless wife I was becoming. My parents' marriage ended in divorce, and I vowed never to let that happen to mine. I was fortunate that Steve did not believe divorce to be an option either. But after nine years, I was stuck asking myself, *Is this it? This is not what I pictured marriage to be. There must be more!* In a sense, the brochure for our cruise of sailing the seven *C*s with my spouse looked a lot more fulfilling than the actual journey was turning out to be!

Now don't get me wrong. Steve and I had our share of good times and special moments. We were set on staying married, and there were definitely times when we said "I love you," although they were few and far between. We fell into the trap of time, family commitments, and not prioritizing God in our relationship. In addition to my full-time job as a middle school principal and Steve's full-time job as an accountant manager for a national transportation company, I taught Sunday school, and Steve was an elder for our church. We both served on church committees or boards and were committed to raising our children in faith. The children were involved in extracurricular activities. We tried to stay healthy and active by exercising. It turns out we were prioritizing everything in our lives except our marriage. There were yearly vacations by ourselves across the country or to a bed-and-breakfast nearby, but these efforts were too few and far between. Business was definitely weakening our marriage. It was nothing like a calm and stress-free cruise!

During our ninth year of marriage, I found myself traveling for work at a conference in San Antonio, Texas. I guess it took the perspective far away from my family in Wisconsin and far away from a place where I thought I'd find guidance—an airport book store—for God to have my attention. In that moment, He drew my focus to a book meant for me entitled *Romancing Your Husband* by Debra White Smith. In that split second, I realized that I had a very one-sided view of marriage: how Steve wasn't making me happy. I was suffering from the "you don't bring me flowers anymore" syndrome. I had never really considered how I might not be meeting his needs. He never complained to me or needed to talk about our marriage like I did. He later admitted he never really realized what was lacking. It seemed to me that he just wanted me to figure it out and quit looking for ways that our marriage wasn't working.

After reflecting on what I read, I realized I was not focused on my contributions to our marriage. I was focused on what I was or was not getting out of our marriage. In that split second, I had my epiphany. If my marriage was going to improve, it was because I decided to change myself and my own actions. Only then, with a selfless heart, could I achieve the marriage of my dreams.

Needless to say, I devoured that book on the plane ride home. I then went into "research mode", reading all I could get my hands on about marriage. The Bible became a source of information and inspiration that God wanted me to have a good marriage and in that I could become a better person. The thing that I realized was the more I focused on meeting Steve's needs, the better I felt about myself and the more fulfilled I became. After a few months, Steve had noticed the change and couldn't help but ask what had happened to me and why was I being so nice to him. My change had inspired him to be a better husband as well.

A year later, I planned a surprise tenth anniversary ceremony where we restated our marriage vows in front of friends and family and afterward set out for a second honeymoon cruise to recommit to our marriage journey. The past eight years have been a direct change of course. Since then, it has been on my heart to continue to research God's plan for marriage and to share it with others. With the assistance of Mark, a friend who leads Bible studies at our church, the concept of "sailing the seven *C*s of marriage" was born. Together, he and I have conducted marriage sessions at our church and have been involved with many couples discussing their marriages.

This book includes many biblical references. You will not need a Bible with you while reading it, but if you have it handy, you will be able to delve deeper into God's Word along the way. As you sail the seven *C*s, don't forget to take time to reflect on how to put the concepts in practice in your marriage. Without taking the time to repair, add on, or maintain your vessel, it will be weakened and compromised in times of hardship as well as in everyday situations. We need to intentionally build a strong vessel that will weather any storm.

As you will see, it is very difficult sailing the journey in the vessel we build without God. At the end of each chapter are reflection exercises to help you mentally and physically grow in your relationship with your spouse as well as in your relationship with God. He is the wind at our sails, and His Word is the course that we chart. But above all, He is the anchor that will keep us steadfast in times of rough weather.

"We have this hope as an anchor for the soul, firm and secure" (Hebrews 6:19).

If you look at an anchor closely, you will see the cross. Thankfully, He is stronger than we would ever need Him to be. We must just remember to rely on Him and trust His might!

I think the ideal approach to working on your marriage is doing so together. Having or downloading two copies of the book so you each can make notes and read at the same time is ideal. If reading it alone, doing the reflection exercises but holding them and waiting to share them with your spouse is also a great plan.

Having said that, remember that *the only person you can truly change is yourself.* You cannot read this book in order to find a way to fix your spouse! Reading this book by yourself can help you gain the insight to work on things within yourself in order to help you become a better spouse. Once you decide that you want the kind of marriage you can look back on later as the trip of a lifetime, remember that only you can make it happen. Once you have made the decision to improve, don't keep it secret. Share your decision with your spouse, and gently see if they are ready to study with you. If so, great! If not, don't worry. Once they see the changes in you and take part in some of the reflection exercises with you, they will want to know more.

Command

But since there is so much immorality, each man should have his own wife, and each woman her own husband.

—1 Corinthians 7:2

We may think that getting married is an essential piece to God's plan for all of us. We read God proclaiming, "Be fruitful and increase in number" (Genesis 1:22). But God wasn't talking to Adam and Eve or any people yet in that statement. He made this proclamation on the fifth day to the animals He created as the rest of the verse says "And fill the water in the seas, and let the birds increase on the earth." He hadn't gotten to us yet.

Of course, much later He does provide guidance to those that marry, but the apostle Paul points out that we will be able to focus more on doing God's work if we choose to remain single. If we are able to control our desires and remain celibate, we will be better able to focus our attention to God and our energy to doing His work. But if we cannot control ourselves, we are *commanded* to marry and have one spouse. According to Paul, "It is good for a man not to marry" (1 Corinthians 7:1). He goes on to say,

> I would like you to be free from concern. An
> unmarried man is concerned about the Lord's
> affairs—how he can please the Lord. But a married
> man is concerned about the affairs of this world—
> how he can please his wife—and his interests are
> divided.

> 1 Corinthians 7:32–35 (NIV)

In the same letter to the Corinthians, he also says to the unmarried and the widows, "It is good for them to stay unmarried, as I am. But if they cannot control themselves, they should marry, for it is better to marry than to burn with passion" 1 Corinthians 7:9. So there it is. Our desire for the opposite sex makes us weak and burn with passion. It is better to marry and have one spouse so that the human passion we burn with can be satisfied. This physical part of marriage is a natural desire that entices us at the beginning and can keep us passionate throughout our relationship. But if you can control this passion, stay single and channel your passion toward doing God's work.

This also implies that it is biblically celebrated if a person does not have sex. Well, that's news in today's culture! It seems that our culture is fixated on sex from every angle and endorses self-gratification however, whenever, and with whomever you can get it. The message today is that we were made to be sexual beings. The truth is that we were made to serve God. But as Paul says, if you burn for desire for that special person and decide to marry, sex will be a celebration of that union. We will look at keeping this passion burning in the fourth *C, couple time,* but more on that later.

Commanded to Become a New Family

God has intentionally created marriage as the union between one man and one woman. Understanding His plan will enable us to better understand our roles as husband and wife within His plan. The Bible says, "For this reason a man will leave his father and mother and be united to his wife and they will become one flesh" (Genesis 2:24). In referring to His creation of Eve as a mate for Adam, God said in Genesis 24:67, "So she became his wife, and he loved her." My personal favorite biblical reference in this area encourages us that this life is not our final paradise anyway, so make the most of it with the person you love.

> Enjoy life with your wife, whom you love, all the days of this meaningless life that God has given you under the sun—all your meaningless days. For this is your lot in life and your toilsome labor under the sun.
>
> Ecclesiastes 9:9 (NIV)

We are told that we will leave the family we know and become a new family with our spouse. We are commanded to build this family in love and that we should enjoy our family. God points out that our life on earth is truly meaningless compared to that which awaits us in heaven, so while we are here and working, He has provided a spouse with whom we can enjoy the fruits of our labor. In this regard, our spouse becomes an escape from labor and our home a refuge at the end of a long day. For some, at this point you may start to see your marriage in a different light and become discouraged. You may feel that your marriage is a source of tension and not an escape from stress at all. I encourage you to keep reading. Then after navigating the rest of the seven *C*s, come back to this first chapter and be encouraged by what God intended for your marriage! I hope you will envision your marriage as a source of pleasure and relaxation, a refuge from the world outside, and a calm cruise to magnificent ports of call.

I can recall a time when my marriage was not a source of relaxation for me, and I have a constant reminder on my kitchen island. My boys were probably six and eight, and as brothers will do, they were bickering over something small that kept growing in intensity. I had a very long day at work and was attempting to put dinner on the table. Steve hadn't come home yet, but I knew when he did, he needed an answer to a decision we were making, and I honestly hadn't had time to think it through. The pressures at work were also demanding my attention, and I felt guilty that I couldn't give attention that night to my children. I felt Steve wouldn't understand this and didn't even think I could share my thoughts and feeling. In my little world, I was feeling pressure from all angles. They boys' argument hit its final crescendo, and I snapped. Spatula in hand, I hit the island with each word that came loudly out of my mouth, "I can't take it anymore!" Our countertops were not granite, but I thought the material was stronger than it turned out to be. That outburst left a nice little gauge on top of the island. The boys stared at me in disbelief. I know they thought I had lost it. When Steve came home, we were all eerily quiet, so he knew something was up. I confessed my outburst and showed him the countertop. It remains in our kitchen to this day as a reminder to me that the problems in life need not get to me and that I should remember that my marriage and my home are a source of rejuvenation, not added stress.

Commanded to Love

Not only are we commanded to build a family together and that this family should bring us joy, we are further commanded to love. Love is actually the highest command God gives to all of us whether young or old, married or single. He says, "And now these three remain: faith, hope and love. But the greatest of these is love" (1 Corinthians

13:13). Paul also tells the Romans in Romans 13:10, "Therefore love is the fulfillment of the Law."

Marriage is the epitome of love, using as its role model Christ's love for the church. Think of marriage as the human example of Jesus's love for all of us as His church. In Jeremiah 2:2, it is written, "I remember the devotions of your youth, how as a bride you loved me and followed me through the desert, through a land not sown." Hosea 3:1 shows the commitment of this love between a husband and a wife through adversity when he writes in Hosea 3:1,

> The Lord said to me, "Go, show your love to your wife again, though she is loved by another and is an adulteress. Love her as the Lord loves the Israelites, though they turn to other gods and love the sacred raisin cakes."

In his letter to the Ephesians 5:23, Paul also writes, "For the husband is the head of the wife as Christ is the head of the church, his body, of which he is the Savior." For God to compare our relationship to our spouse as the closest thing to His relationship to us, His church, gives great meaning to the way we are to treat each other in marriage. Think of the love we are to show each other as the example of God's love to us—the highest love there is. In the diagram below, marriage is the greatest display of God's love for us.

Marriage Love

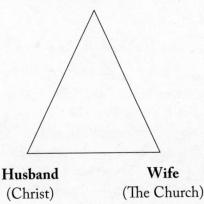

| **Husband** | **Wife** |
| (Christ) | (The Church) |

Commanded in Our Roles as Husband and Wife

As we strive to love each other, we have been given different roles as husband and wife. Before exploring these roles, we need to consider our personalities. Each one of us is uniquely different according to the gifts God has given us. Even though the husband is the head of the wife, many women have been gifted with strong abilities in leadership. I have been a secondary school administrator at the high school and middle school level for seventeen years. You cannot be a pushover or lack vision to do those jobs. At home, however, I need to allow my husband, Steve, to be the "head of the household" and support and empower him in this role. Stick with me, I'll show you why this is so important and how much power the wife has in supporting her husband!

The Role of the Husband

The husband is in the image of Christ. He is the spiritual and physical leader of the home. He is charged by God to love and cherish his wife. There can only be one true leader in a relationship. Any organization with more than one leader is destined to be in conflict. As our ultimate leader, Jesus shows us that He is a servant leader, loving us with all of His heart and willing to die for us. That is what a leader does—puts himself on the line to ensure that those who depend on him will thrive. In his letter to the Colossians 3:19, Paul writes, "Husbands, love your wives and do not be harsh with them." The Apostle Peter too shows husbands that a true leader is gracious and caring to those he leads:

> Husbands, in the same way be considerate as you live with your wives, and treat them with respect as the weaker partner and heirs with you of the gracious gift of life, so that nothing will hinder your prayers.

> 1 Peter 3:7 (NIV)

Wait a second, ladies. I know what you're thinking. "I will not be seen as the weaker partner in my marriage!" Think of it this way. I think that from little girls on, we envision the man of our dreams as our knight in shining armor that sweeps us off our feet. He is strong and confident in his abilities and is a leader others look up to. This is the kind of strength God is talking about, not abusive strength or bullying strength. We must build our husband up into the confident leader God needs in order for him to guide our marriage and our family with integrity and good intentions.

As the husband is the leader of the family, he is also commanded to be respectful and loving toward his wife. Why does God command this? He commands this because it doesn't always come naturally to a man. I'm sure we all know husbands that have said, "I told her that I loved her on our wedding day, and if it changes, I'll let her know. So I don't need to tell her that I still love her—she already knows." Women need to feel loved and cherished just like we as the church need to know that Christ loves us no matter what happens, no matter what we look like, and no matter what may come our way. Husbands need to remember that women crave the feeling of being loved, cherished, and secured just as we crave this feeling from Christ. The more women feel this security, the warmer and more responsive they become.

As a leader, you want those that you are in charge of to feel safe and secure in your leadership. This does not come from coercion or threats. This comes from a genuine respect for and empowerment of others, building others up so that they can become their best. Never does my husband appear stronger to me than when he is at his gentlest, most caring state. Treating others with compassion does require a sense of power and control in that you have it and choose to put it aside for the time being. Jesus did this time and again when He let others come to Him in His compassion and seek from Him what they needed.

When a leader humbles himself to others, he creates the desire for others to follow him, and a leader is only a leader when those that follow do so of their free will. Otherwise the "leader" is in reality a dictator using force, and followers truly do not have a choice.

The Role of the Wife

The wife is in the image of the church. She is to submit and obey in the marriage relationship. These two words, *submit* and *obey*, have been used and misused so often that they evoke a very negative connotation to young couples looking to build a marriage based on equality. Some women have had it so engrained in them that a man should not rule over them, that they bring this independent attitude and power with them into marriage, and thus power struggles and conflict ensue. Pride can get in the way of the wife's submission just as it can for the husband in terms of sacrifice. Both have been given different roles in the marriage, but both are perfectly equal and Christ-like ways of following Jesus by walking in love as children imitating the God who is love.

God did not intend for the wife not to have input or opinions in the family. It's quite the opposite, as most husbands will confess that they value their wife's thoughts and opinions and use the wife's input as guidance on most issues. It takes the realization that you have power in the relationship in order to submit that power to your spouse. This is true in our relationship with God as well. As human beings, we have free will and the power to satisfy our needs and desires. We are asked by God to submit this often to serve Him and others and not ourselves. Listen to how God commands the wife through Paul in Colossians 3:18: "Wives, submit to your husbands, as it is fitting in the Lord." It is also stated in Ephesians 5:24: "Now as the church submits to Christ, so also wives should submit to their husbands in everything."

We are to give our input and then support our husbands in the final decisions with all of our strength. Our husbands are human. They will not always make the right decision. But if they feel empowered by their wife, the two will grow closer as a team. God realized, however, that a team (or a sailing ship in this case) can only have one captain in order to be successful.

Let's be honest. A woman wants a strong and confident leader in her husband. He will not reach his potential in this area if she stands in his way or cuts down his decisions. Remember the knight in shining armor? How will he feel if his wife comes barreling in on a bigger horse with a larger sword? His confidence will be shaken, and he will grow weaker in his ability to make a decision. As a woman builds up and supports her husband, his strength grows, and he has the willingness and confidence to lead their family. With this strength, as mentioned before, comes the increased ability if he so chooses to be gentle and caring toward his wife. A wife carries a great deal of power over her husband. She must choose to submit in order to strengthen her husband and enjoy the security and love that his strength will provide. Paul informs women of this power in Ephesians 5:33: "However, each one of you also must love his wife as he loves himself, and the wife must respect her husband."

A woman is then charged to respect her husband. Just as love and gentleness does not always come easy for a man, respecting and supporting her husband does not always come easy for a woman. In submitting and building up her husband, a wife will be praised. God wanted wives to work toward this relationship as the payoff is great. This is further explained in the epilogue to the book of Proverbs where twenty-two verses all speak to "the wife of noble character." The wife described is by no means weak or helpless. She is strong, and her value is evident. Listen to the description of and rewards for such a wife.

> A wife of noble character who can find? She is worth far more than rubies. Her husband has full confidence in her and lacks nothing of value. She brings him good, not harm, all the days of her life. She selects wool and flax and works with eager hands. She is like the merchant ships, bringing her food from afar. She gets up while it is still dark; she

provides food for her family and portions for her servant girls. She considers a field and buys it; out of her earning she plants a vineyard. She sets about her work vigorously; her arms are strong for her tasks. She sees that her trading is profitable, and her lamp does not go out at night. In her hand she holds the distaff and grasps the spindle with her fingers. She opens her arms to the poor and extends her hands to the needy. When it snows, she has no fear for her household; for all of them are clothed in scarlet. She makes coverings for her bed; she is clothed in fine linen and purple. Her husband is respected at the city gate, where he takes his seat among the elders of the land. She makes linen garments and sells them, and supplies the merchants with sashes. She is clothed with strength and dignity; she can laugh at the days to come. She speaks with wisdom, and faithful instructions on her tongue. She watches over the affairs of her household and does not eat the bread of idleness. Her children arise and class her blessed; her husband also, and he praises her; "Many women do noble things, but you surpass them all." Charm is deceptive, and beauty is fleeting; but a woman who fears the Lord is to be praised. Give her the reward she has earned, and let her works bring her praise at the city gate.

Proverbs 31:10–31 (NIV)

This does not sound to me like a weak, feeble woman who lets herself be ruled by her husband! Instead, the wife of noble character is a strong and confident woman who contributes to her family in many ways. Her husband realizes and values the contributions of his wife and praises her along with others. Consider this as the relationship between Christ and the church. In this relationship, we see that Jesus in the role of the husband values a hardworking church that does not sit by and wait for things to happen but makes things happen. We are commanded to be hardworking, creative, and effective in order to spread the works and Word of God to others. The wife, acting as the church, has a crucial role in the success of the marriage, and the wife of noble character knows this.

With this kind of wife, a husband can feel empowered to lead, and the union or the team created sails on a solid foundation. Each spouse becomes confident in the role they were commanded to have in the relationship meant to be an example of the epitome of love on earth.

Chapter 1
Reflection Activity:
Fulfilling the Command

Fulfilling our role for the kind of husband and wife God wants us to be does not come without conscious effort and understanding. Having a grasp of what you are currently doing well and in what areas you would like to improve will help you become the spouse you want to be.

1. Write down words or phrases that define/describe what kind of husband or wife you want to be.

2. Identify areas you are strong in right now.

3. Identify areas in which you wish to improve.

4. Discuss with your spouse your description of an ideal marriage. You may have similarities and differences in your definition of *ideal*. Remember that you cannot change anyone but yourself, so through that lens, what things would you both begin to work on in your marriage?

5. Prayer:

   Lord, You have given us a command that if we are not to be alone, to be in a sacred union with the one we have chosen. Thank You for Your gift of marriage and for the ability and privilege to become one flesh with another person. You intended this to be a wonderful unity that would strengthen the two of us. Help us to clearly envision the ideal relationship You have in store for us and help us each do what we can to reach that ideal. In Jesus's name we pray, amen.

This is the strong vessel we are commanded to build in order to withstand the other *C*s we have to negotiate. Let's sail further!

Commitment

For this reason a man will leave his father and mother and be united to his wife, and the two will become one flesh. This is a profound mystery—but I am talking about Christ and the church.

—Ephesians 5:31–32

I have to admit that my number one fear in life is drowning. I get more than mildly freaked out at the thought of swimming without a life jacket in the middle of a deep lake, and I made it through the lifesaving course at the YMCA! So it struck me as funny when I realized that my perfect marriage analogy would be sailing with my partner through the vast seas of life! When contemplating my fear of water, I also realized that my greatest stress reliever in life is being on the beach, watching the water, and enjoying the calming pattern of incoming and outgoing waves. Maybe you're like me. A tranquil setting on or near water can soothe you and bring you joy, but an endless ocean causes panic. In the end, it's a great analogy for marriage. We want to commit to a life of calm and tranquility. We don't want uncertainty, struggle, or fear to enter. But enter it will. And we must *commit* to marriage in its entirety, like Christ *committed* to us, not to just the good times.

The Definition of Love

As Jesus committed His life to the church and ultimately sacrificed Himself for us, think about the depth of this commitment and how we need to put our spouse before ourselves. Why is this serving our spouse and putting him first so difficult? Let's take a look at what God intended love to be. Many couples use the following verse during their wedding ceremony but forget the words soon after.

> Love is patient, love is kind. It does not boast, it is not proud. It is not rude, it is not self-seeking, it is not easily angered, it keeps no record of wrongs. Love does not delight in evil but rejoices with the truth. It always protects, always trusts, always hopes, always perseveres.
>
> 1 Corinthians 13:4–7 (NIV)

We are told that love is the most important thing in life, greater in fact than faith and hope. So if we are to enact love the way God intended, we are to put aside every need and desire we have and look to serve others with patience, kindness, calmness, truthfulness, and courage. If we commit to following the words of God, we commit not only to His definition of love, but also to His definition of holy living.

> Put to death, therefore, whatever belongs to your earthly nature: sexual immorality, impurity, lust, evil desires and greed, which is idolatry. Because of these, the wrath of God is coming. You used to walk

in these way, in the life you once lived. But now you must rid yourselves of all such things as these: anger, rage, malice, slander and filthy language from your lips. Do not lie to each other, since you have taken off your old self with its practices and have put on the new self, which is being renewed in knowledge in the image of its Creator.

Colossians 3:5–10 (NIV)

Your commitment to God and to your spouse is a very mature and conscious decision. You are promising to put your needs behind the needs of others, especially the one person you have committed yourself to for life. This is the essence of love: self-emptying that ends up fulfilling. You only get what you give away; you lose what you keep. In this light, we imitate God by being servants to one another. In his book *Covenant Marriage*, Gary Chapman asserts that "man by nature is self-centered, and the desire for a lifelong marriage usually focuses on the individual's realization that that is best for him or her. However, such self-centered thinking is not what produces lifelong marriages" (Chapman, p. 28).

When you and your spouse first decided to get married, you probably felt that nothing in this world could ever separate you. All you wanted to do was to spend time together. When Steve and I met, we lived two hours apart, and sometimes I was tired when I got in the car to go visit him. But all I would have to do was to pull out his picture, set it on the seat next to me, and glance at it now and then.

Magically, the fatigue left me, and the butterflies set in. *How could anything ever get in the way of these feelings?* I thought. I was naive. After a few years of marriage, I was hard-pressed to find a picture of him in my wallet or later on my cell phone!

Yes, life got in the way of my commitment. The sailing team we had formed on our wedding day seemed to falter from lack of practice on the fundamentals and lack of commitment to each other. We were, in effect, beginning to sail on two separate journeys. The life we started together diminished as our separate lives got busier. As I was still working, I wore many "hats"—mother, boss, colleague, daughter, sister, Sunday school teacher and so on—each role demanding more of my time. Each role I added seemed to take more and more out of me until I had very little to give to my husband. Everything else appeared to be more important than the role of wife. Deep inside, both Steve and I knew we needed to prioritize each other; we just weren't sure why or how.

Contract vs. Commitment

As discussed earlier, society has us programmed to believe that love involves a focus on ourselves and how we can be happy. When we feel our needs are not being met, it makes us feel justified to become disgruntled and even, eventually, to move on. We look at our marriages today more like contracts instead of commitments. In a contract, two parties draw up their own needs and legally agree to the deal. If one of the parties does not meet the stipulations of the other or does not fulfill their end of the bargain, the contract has been broken. The other party therefore feels justified to dissolve the contract as it doesn't seem like their fault the deal has gone bad in the first place.

In this light, I look at my marriage through a me-centered lens. My roles become paramount in my view of life, and if my partner cannot understand what I am going through, how to ease my burden, make me feel special, or anticipate my needs, then I'm not happy with him. The contract mentality states that I have the "right" to be satisfied or "my money back." It implies that I should keep score or keep track of my needs being met or the deal is off. Yes, there is that part about me meeting the needs of my spouse, but if they aren't meeting my needs, why even need to try?

Instead, we need to view our marriage commitment the way that God does. His term for commitment is *covenant*. The weight of the word *covenant* is not to be taken lightly. When writing his book *Covenant Marriage*, Gary Chapman refers to the word *covenant* as being different than a contract in that it is "initiated for the benefit of the other person" (Chapman, p. 13), is built on "unconditional promises" (Chapman, p. 15), is "based on steadfast love" (Chapman, p. 17), is "viewed as permanent" (Chapman, p. 20), and "requires confrontation and forgiveness" (Chapman, p. 21).

God uses this word six times in the Bible to emphasize His commitment to the church. In the situations where He is using the word *covenant*, God is making a binding promise, and His presence remains in that promise. Consider the covenants (or commitments or promises) that God has made chronologically:

> Then God said to Noah and to his sons with him: "I now establish my covenant with you and with your descendants after you and with every living creature that was with you—the birds, the livestock and all the wild animals, all those that came out of the ark with you—every living creature on earth. I establish my covenant with you: Never again will all life be cut off by the waters of a flood; never again will there be a flood to destroy the earth."
>
> Genesis 9:8–11 (NIV)

> Then Moses went up to God, and the Lord called to him from the mountain and said, "This is what you are to say to the house of Jacob and what you are to tell the people of Israel: You yourselves have seen what I did to Egypt, and how I carried you on eagles' wings and brought you to myself. Now if you obey me fully and keep my covenant, then out of all nations you will be my treasured possession. Although the whole earth is mine, you will be for me a kingdom of priests and a holy nation. These are the words you are to speak to the Israelites."
>
> Exodus 19:3–6 (NIV)

"The time is coming," declares the Lord, "when I will make a new covenant with the house of Israel and with the house of Judah. It will not be like the covenant I made with their forefathers when I took them by the hand to lead them out of Egypt, because they broke my covenant, though I was a husband to them" declares the Lord. This is the covenant I will make with the house of Israel after that time," declares the Lord. "I will put my law in their minds and write it on their hearts. I will be their God, and they will be my people."

Jeremiah 31:31–33 (NIV)

In the same way, after supper he took the cup, saying, "This cup is the new covenant in my blood; do this, whenever you drink it, in remembrance of me."

1 Corinthians 11:25 (NIV)

These things may be taken figuratively, for the women represent two covenants. One covenant is from Mount Sinai and bears children who are to be slaves; This is Hagar.... Now you, brothers, like Isaac, are children of promise.... Therefore, brothers, we are not children of the slave woman, but of the free woman.

Galatians 4:24, 28, 31 (NIV)

For this reason Christ is the mediator of a new covenant, that those who are called may receive the promised eternal inheritance—now that he has died as a ransom to set them free from the sins committed under the first covenant.

Hebrews 9:15 (NIV)

You made a covenant or commitment on your wedding day to your spouse, who was everything you ever wanted at the time. After a while, we tend to see the faults of our spouse more clearly, and they cloud the picture of the perfect mate we used to have. There are many things we'd like to change in our spouse in order to help him or her become a better person or be better suited to us. But just imagine, as you are thinking of what you'd like to change in your spouse, your spouse may be thinking about what they would like to change in you! In the end, it is crucial to understand that we have made a commitment to the person our spouse *is* and not to the person we think he or she can be.

Because we are human, we are not perfect and make mistakes. A key part of remembering a commitment is forgiveness. Sometimes our spouse knows exactly what action has upset us. Sometimes he or she has no clue. Harboring the anger or resentment we are supposed to let go of can eat us up inside to the point of forming a wedge between us and our spouse. Because we are human, we will make many mistakes and need forgiveness countless times. Thankfully, our Father in heaven forgives us over and over again. If our marriage is to mirror that of Christ and the church, we must show this same forgiveness to our spouse. After all, we are told in Matthew 18:22 to forgive each other not seven but "seventy-seven times." Paul also tells us to "be kind and compassionate to one another, forgiving each other, just as in Christ God forgave you" (Ephesians 4:32).

In marriage, you have the following options when severe trouble comes your way: you can divorce, you can live miserably, or you can honor your commitment and go through healing and reconciliation. Imagine if God chose to break His covenants to His people and left His church! He has given us examples of how strong His promises are in order for us to have the courage to hold on to our promises. God calls us to be joined as one flesh. This is an image of a union that could not or should not be separated!

> For this reason a man will leave his father and mother and be united to his wife, and the two will become one flesh. This is a profound mystery—but I am talking about Christ and the church.
>
> Ephesians 5:31–32 (NIV)

The saying goes that we are hardest to love when we need it the most. In those times, I remember that my spouse is a child of God, created in His image just as I am. God made Him the exact way He wanted him to be, and He loves Steve more than I ever can. When I look at him in this light, his weaknesses are overshadowed by his strengths, and I remember why I grew to love him in the first place.

I remember the commitment I made to him, and my heart softens. Sometimes this process is instantaneous. Sometimes it takes a little longer. It also helps when I remember my own imperfections and the need for Steve to forgive me as well as I am not perfect. In Matthew 7:3, we are told not to judge or we too will be judged: "Why do you look at the speck of sawdust in your brother's eye and pay no attention to the plank in your own eye?"

We vow, promise, or commit at the time of marriage to love each other in sickness, health, wealth, poverty, good times, bad times, and even until death. Those are promises of an unending commitment and not of a legally binding contract. Those are the conditions that we want God to love His church under and never leave us. Those are the words that will carry a vessel through many miles of calm as well as turbulent waters.

Chapter 2
Reflection Activity:
Renewing the Commitment

1. Remember your wedding day and reflect upon the characteristics of your spouse that you most admired.

2. Write down the things you wish you could change about your spouse. Now take that paper, tear it into tiny pieces, and throw it away. Remember that you

have committed to your husband or wife just the way he or she is.

3. Complete the Commitment Pledge in Appendix A. You can rip the page out of the back of the book or download it for your spouse. After completing the Commitment Pledge, sign it and give it to your spouse, reading it to them if you are able.

4. Prayer:

Lord, You created us in your image, commanded us to marry if we needed to, and provided for us a spouse to respect, cherish, and love. We have made an everlasting commitment to our spouse. Help us understand this commitment, and give us words and actions to say and do as evidence of the commitment we have made. In Jesus's name we pray, amen.

Communication

Everyone should be quick to listen, slow to speak and slow to become angry, for man's anger does not bring about the righteous life that God desires.

—James 1:19–20

Imagine sailing on your lifelong journey and not being able to communicate about your thoughts, feelings, or struggles with your shipmate. You are stuck negotiating the waters by yourself. You are, in essence, two ships passing in the night. Communication is essential to a fulfilling, exciting, and even relaxing journey.

Many years ago on the show *Saturday Night Live*, there was a skit with a husband and wife going out to eat at an upscale restaurant. They were seated by a waiter in black tie, who politely pushed the chair in for the woman. He then handed the couple thin black menus that looked like the wine list. The couple started discussing their options: "So," said the wife, "would you like to talk about the weather or the political climate of Russia?" "Well," answered her husband, "I was leaning more toward the big game on Sunday."

The fancy menus turned out to be menus for conversation! It appears the couple had run out of things to talk about and needed to be handed talking points to prompt them. After they selected their conversation, the waiter brought them details and questions under the chosen topic. While watching this, I thought to my unmarried self, *Wow, could a marriage really get to that point? Mine won't!*

Years later, my married self remembered that skit. I knew that Steve and I rarely had time to talk anymore between our schedules and the kids. I decided to count how many words we would say to each other on a particular day. The answer: twelve! We had spoken twelve words to each other that day! We were finding less and less chances to connect as a couple, and when we did have the opportunity, like at the dinner table, we weren't taking it. We were letting the children dominate the conversation and didn't have the energy to initiate one ourselves.

The next chance we had to go out to eat by ourselves, I made it a point to have deep and meaningful conversations preplanned. My poor husband was looking forward to a nice, relaxing meal without children, and what he walked into probably felt to him like an interrogation by the FBI. "What quality do you appreciate the most in me?" "If you could select another career at this point in your life, what would it be?" "Where would you most like our family to travel together?" After the third conversation, I could tell I better not push my luck as he was getting a bit agitated, so I went back to asking him how he liked his steak.

We have all seen different communication scenarios take place in marriages. There may be talking, but it is very heavily one-sided by the wife. Women by nature are generally wired to talk more, and their husbands find it difficult to keep up at times. In the end, a husband may begin to tune out his wife. He may think he can fake it pretty well most of the time, but others can see right through his charade. In some marriages, the husband may be more verbally dominant, and I know many couples where this is the case. Whichever spouse it may be, he or she may not be aware of the percentage of the conversation they are dominating over his or her spouse.

None of us go into marriage thinking that our spouse is someone we really don't want to talk to. As time goes by and we have made different communication mistakes with our spouse, we tend to get gun-shy and hold our tongues. We learn we shouldn't assume his intentions, have an answer for every hypothetical question, or avoid our spouse when something is obviously wrong, hoping that it will fade in time. But we may not understand the background to consider when talking to our spouse whose communication style may be different than our own.

In order to effectively communicate information with your spouse, you need to understand four things: the *filters* they bring to communication, their *communication style*, the *levels of communication*, and your spouse's "*love language*" (Chapman). It may sound complicated, but understanding where you are each coming from and where you want to go when communicating to each other will be easy and helpful. After looking at communicating information, we will then look at how to communicate love to your spouse.

Communication Filters

We come at life from different places, different backgrounds, and different familial influences. These experiences make us who we are and how we see the world. They also help to formulate how we will be perceived by and relate to others with different experiences. To visually represent this concept, think of a large funnel. Messages come in from the outside and pass through many layers as we strive to make meaning of them for ourselves. The way I filter a message may be very different from how Steve filtered the same message. If Steve is sending the message, the way I interpret it may be very different than the way he intended it.

Your Communication Filter

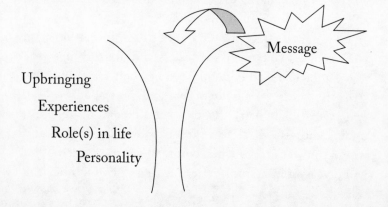

Upbringing
   Experiences
      Role(s) in life
         Personality

Message

Upbringing

Your first step in processing is your upbringing and the role models you had at home. Maybe you lived in a home where most members of the family freely talked to each other and held little back. Personal issues were discussed around the dinner table, and everyone assisted with the problem solving. This could have been done in a loud, boisterous fashion or could have been low-key and calm. Coming from either environment may make you eager to share thoughts and feelings with those you love and trust.

You may have come from a loving environment in which attention was focused on you as the most important person speaking at the time. Your needs, thoughts, and issues were held in high esteem and attended to as soon as possible. You may have grown accustomed to being the center of attention and learned at an early age how to captivate and entertain an audience. Your experience could have been the complete opposite, however. If there was a family dinnertime, it may have often been quiet where everyone was consumed by their own thoughts but didn't dare speak them aloud. Conversation may have been very matter-of-fact and included what was on the agenda for the next day and who needed to be picked up when. Your parents' relationship may have been intact but noncommunicative, or they may have had many issues and chose to be less verbal with each other. In any case, these were your role models for the future.

Many of us may come from either single-parent or broken homes, which added a layer of complexity to communication. One parent had to come from both angles of mother and father, which is difficult or impossible for many to handle consistently. There may have been anger, resentment, apathy, or exhaustion playing large roles in the way a parent or guardian communicated with the children. Those who we looked up to may have been doing the best they felt they could with the situation they had, and we may or may not have been able to share information and process it effectively under those circumstances.

It is important to realize that the situations we are faced with early on in life do have a great impact on our own approach to communication. They should not, however, become an excuse for us once we are adults and see that there are other ways to approach speaking and listening. If we have had experiences that have shaped the way we communicate in a dysfunctional way, it is up to us to learn and build upon alternative skills. If we realize we have to work on patience in listening, being slow to anger, sharing attention, or opening up to others, we must do so. "When I was a child, I talked like a child, I thought like a child, I reasoned like a child. When I became a man, I put childish ways behind me" (1 Corinthians 13:11).

"A wise man's heart guides his mouth, and his lips promote instruction" (Proverbs 16:23).

Roles in Life

The roles that we play in our lives may also have an effect on how we approach communication with others, including our spouse. If you are in a position of power, authority or decision making, you may find it difficult to break out of this mode when at home. When people look to you for answers all day long, you may find yourself in a problem-solving mode of quick processing and logical (to you at least) fixes that may work great at work, but not so well with a spouse who may need more processing time with issues that don't have quick fixes.

You may have a role whether on a job or as a volunteer or as a family member where you are caring for others. This role demands a great deal of patience and energy. It may make you increasingly sensitive to the needs of others, or on the flip side, it may drain you and leave you with almost nothing left to give. Coming home to a spouse who may desire your attention may be the last thing you have the strength for. You may be in a role where you are researching and thinking all day long, and by the end of the day, you are mentally exhausted. You may need to rejuvenate through physical activity, or you may yearn for brainless downtime. Still others may be in physically demanding roles where they are drained of all energy. Regardless of what we do, when we communicate with our spouse, what we hear passes through another layer of our filter as far as the role we have played that day. It may be difficult not to see our spouse through the lens we have been using. Our spouse is not in the role of a coworker, supervisor, community member, volunteer leader, etc. He is in the role of our partner, and we must adjust ourselves mentally and physically when in communication with the most important person in our lives.

As you filter communication from your spouse, the last level to consider is your personality as well as his or hers. There are many personality tests out there that you may or may not be aware of. After answering questions, you are categorized as having certain psychological traits and then receive an interpretation of how these traits define your thoughts, words, actions, and general approach to the world. Here are a few you can find:

- ◄ The Myers Briggs Type Indicator compares you on scales of extroverted or introverted (do you get your energy from other people or from your own internal world?), sensing or intuitive (do you focus on the present and what you can see, or the future and what you can imagine?), thinking or feeling (do you make decisions based on logic or on values and people?), and judging or perceiving (do you prefer things structured and organized or flexible and spontaneous?). (http://www.personalitydesk.com/product/mbti-step-i-interpretive-report?gclid=COrNoO_HrK0CFYvDKgodnx5hkw)

≺ Peter Bender's assessments looks in what quadrant you are most of the time. The quadrants are based on traits including how you act and react to situations, if you are drawn more to tasks or people, and whether you speak in questions or answers. The quadrants include typing you as "analytical, amiable, expressive, or driver." (http://www.peterursbender. com/quiz/swtable.html)

≺ Gary Smalley and Dr. John Trent classify personality in terms of animals we can relate to when looking at personality. You fit into one of four categories: lion (dominance), otter (influence), beaver (compliance), or retriever (steadiness).

The goal of such personality tests is to see how you psychologically tend to approach others and, thus, situations. If you approach communication with a task-oriented, problem-solving mentality and your spouse approaches it from a people-oriented, feeling perspective, you may be worlds apart in interpreting the words of the other person. Being aware of our unique personality styles and how this affects how we not only communicate but also process communication will help us in thinking through our approach with our spouse. This is a valuable tool in whatever role we play in the world, but a critical tool in our role as a husband or wife. If you realize you need to give your spouse more time to think and react, it will help you have patience because you understand this need. If your partner knows you make judgments based on feelings, they can help by understanding this before providing you with more analytical information and details.

Communication Styles: Male and Female

Much has been written about the differences between men and women. Like all stereotypes, please keep in mind that the generalizations can be made because *most* men and *most* women can be described in these generalities. However, there are men and women who do not fit the gender stereotype in this and other areas. So as you read, consider that you are by no means "abnormal" if this does not apply to you!

I have heard it reported that men have the ability to think about nothing. They can shut all thought processes down and simply focus on absolutely nothing! In his research for his video series Laugh Your Way to a Better Marriage, pastor, author, and speaker Mark Gungor refers to this as the nothing box. He asserts that men's brains organize information into boxes and that never do these boxes touch. There is a box for wife, kids, work, sex, garage, mother-in-law, etc., but a man's favorite box is the "nothing box," which he will take out and open in his brain as often as possible as a form of stress relief and relaxation.

He refers to women's brains as a ball of wire in which everything is connected to everything else and where details about seemingly unrelated things can be accessed at a moment's notice. Pam and Bill Farrel, in their 2007 book *Men Are Like Waffles—Women Are Like Spaghetti*, use this same concept in food picture form. The individual segments in a waffle are separated and never touch, but a plate of spaghetti seems infinitely connected.

Both concepts essentially state that men focus on one topic or issue at a time and have difficulty shifting from that one topic as there are barriers to that kind of transitional thinking. Women, on the other hand, have no barriers to their thinking and process many topics simultaneously, thus enabling them to multitask with ease. I am not saying that as women we multitask perfectly, but I can tell you that we can get a lot of things half-done in no time!

When I was first introduced to this concept, I decided to try it out on Steve. We were on a long car ride, and I turned to him as we were passing cornfield after cow pasture and asked him what he was thinking about. "Nothing" was his answer. The boys, not yet teens at the time, found this fascinating, so I'm wondering when this ability in men develops to its fullest potential. We pressed Steve further to confirm that he was literally thinking of nothing as certainly he had to be thinking of our final destination, when and where to stop for gas, how blessed he is to have such an awesome family—anything? But nope, he convinced us that he was truly thinking of nothing. A little while later, I turned and asked him the same question.

This time he answered that he considered it odd for the cow we just passed to be standing the way it was. That's when I realized he did really have a nothing box.

It is extremely difficult for me as a woman to dream that I could seriously sit and think about nothing. Something always seems to be in the way, especially at night. I think that's why ads for sleeping pills generally show women as we have the most problems shutting off our brains. As something is always happening within us mentally, it often needs to be processed verbally in order to have sense made of it. This is why women as a whole are much more verbal than men. The need to verbalize is due to the amount of processing through issues that they need to do. Think of it as untangling a wadded up mess of Christmas lights. Until they are straightened out, it is hard to make sense of which strand goes where. Women process information verbally, make lists, and leave themselves physical clues to separate the strands in their minds. To a woman, it is a very valuable process.

Men, on the other hand, process one issue at a time until it is worked out. They don't often need to process with others unless they are stuck on a single concept or detail. When their spouse asks them to talk about what is bugging them, they are reluctant to do so if it isn't fully worked out in their own mind yet as doing so would confuse the issue.

These two different ways of processing information internally and verbally can lead to misunderstandings and frustrations. A wife may feel her husband is hiding things from her or doesn't value her opinion enough to share things with her. A husband may feel his wife shares too much with him and others and violates their privacy or dwells on issues too long. If both spouses don't understand how the other is thinking, other stereotypes like the nagging wife or the distant husband can come into play. In Proverbs 19:13, the Bible paints another picture of how a wife's attempt at communication over and over may appear to her husband: "And a quarrelsome wife is like a constant dripping."

Husbands, understand that your wife may need to verbally process with you and that for a time she may need your undivided attention. After you have listened attentively and helped her process, you will have made her feel valued and validated. Wives, understand that your husband may need some time alone to work out his own issues or to just relax and get away from his issues. This time is precious to him. By allowing him the time and not getting angry or jealous, you will help him know that you respect his need to be alone so that he can be a better husband when you come back together.

Levels of Communication

Sometimes I just want to talk to Steve to communicate that I had a very difficult day. I need him to understand my mood and how I need to work through some things. I'm not looking for his opinions or problem-solving input at that time; I just want to tell. Other times I am truly wanting him to sit and look me in the eye and offer his insights and opinions on what I'm thinking about. He has approached me at different times with different needs as well. Unless we are explicit with each other and tell each other what level of communication we want to initiate, the other is left guessing. We have learned to say things like "I just need to tell you what happened today" or "We need to make a decision together on this" so that we are on the same page.

Information that you share with your spouse can and should be as simple as the facts about your day or their day, how the weather is affecting things, or what the latest information is in the neighborhood. But it should also get to topics involving your spouse's thoughts about what is happening politically, how they interpret a certain Bible passage, or what their thoughts are about a certain movie review. And finally, as a couple, we should also be frequently getting to such topics as how your spouse felt about something you said, or what they thought about your actions in a certain situation and why. Getting to the depths of feelings and emotions requires trust in your marriage. It also requires practice.

In his book *Covenant Marriage*, Gary Chapman asserts that there are five levels of communication: hallway talk, reporter talk, intellectual talk, emotional talk, and loving truth talk (Chapman, p. 51). I picture the levels as a descending staircase.

As you step down to the next level, you reach further into a person's heart and soul. Each level requires an increased level of trust and vulnerability with your partner. At the top of the communication staircase, we are sharing surface-level insights about the weather or something trivial. Going a little deeper, we begin to share about our day or an event to let the other person know facts about the topic. Next come our thoughts and opinions on events or topics that let the other person know a little more about our viewpoints. Going down again, we begin to share how we are feeling, and finally we get to the point of sharing our fears, dreams, and insecurities.

Most of our communication as couples and as society in general stays safely in the first three levels. We feel very comfortable usually communicating facts, events, or stories, and oftentimes we throw our opinion about something into the mix. When pressed for how we are truly feeling about something, however, we share those ideas only with those we feel safe with. Unless we share our feelings on a somewhat regular basis, it may become difficult to get to this level, even with those that we love.

We may find ourselves sharing more details on certain topics with friends or coworkers than we do our spouse. We may spend more time with them during the day and have more opportunity for conversation, or by the end of the day, we simply forget. How many times have you and your spouse been involved in conversation with others when one of you turns to the other and says, "You never told me that!" We then have to retreat back in our memory because we are sure we wouldn't have withheld that information from our spouse, but sure enough, we just forgot about it!

In the age of instant messaging, Steve and I have found it easy to communicate a "teaser" message to each other via e-mail or text message so that we put it on "the list" to talk about later. Yes, this does bring up the memory of the conversation menu, but this time we are putting the topics on. The key is making time later to discuss what is on the list. We have found that we need to have no distractions— no television, electronic devices, children, etc.—to be able to open up to each other what our true feelings are. This makes the conversation more fulfilling, a decision a pleasant consensus, and we both come away better for having the conversation.

Communicating Love

We have been looking into how we as a married couple communicate information to each other verbally. This is crucial in having an effective marriage. I would argue that another aspect of communication is even more important: communicating your love for your spouse. You may think you are already doing this by periodically telling your spouse that you love him or her. Even though he is hearing the words, he may not be seeing or feeling your love, and therefore the words become empty and meaningless. Communicating by an affirming message, physical symbol, time, and/or action love to your spouse will help to make your marriage even more fulfilling.

In his book *The Five Love Languages*, Gary Chapman offers that each of us feel loved and validated in different ways. Some of us respond to words of affirmation or verbal validations of what we have done or who we are (Chapman, p. 39). Letting your spouse know that you are proud of them, that they look great, or that they did a great job on something specific helps them know that you are paying attention and therefore leads them to feel loved. Notes, e-mails, or text messages that affirm are all great ways to meet the needs of a spouse with this love language.

The other love languages include having quality time by prioritizing them by spending time engaged in each other's presence (Chapman, p. 59), giving gifts as physical symbols of your love (Chapman, p. 81), providing acts of service by doing something for the other person that will help them out (Chapman, p. 97), or physical touch by reaching out and touching them—yes, this does include intimacy (Chapman, p. 115). Rarely do spouses share the same love language, which makes it difficult to connect. One spouse thinks he is communicating love when he is doing so in ways that he wants, not in ways that his wife may respond to. We are called again to not focus on our own needs but on the needs of our spouse. In the Bible, the Lord said to Moses, "Love your neighbor as yourself" (Leviticus 19:18).

I would argue that God wants us to consider that each of us is different and want to be loved in the ways that make us feel special. We are to find out what our spouse needs from us and provide it to them. Gary Chapman has written many books based on the love languages, and each one comes with an assessment that you and your spouse can take to identify what you value. You can also do this research at home by conducting experiments of words, actions, quality time, physical touch, and small gifts on your own and finding out what is appreciated most by your spouse. Your "research" should bring with it great reward as you look to draw closer as a couple. Without knowing that I value quality time and physical touch, Steve tried hard to get me just the right gift to express how he felt about me. Little did he know this love language was the lowest on my scale! When we started spending more time together and sharing more hugs, he realized what I needed from him in order to feel loved. I started noticing that the more I could be of service to him and help him with his to-do list and the more affirmation I could verbalize to him, the more valued I made him feel.

Differences in the way we communicate and process information and love can lead to dashed expectations and conflict. Understanding your and your spouse's communication filters, style, love language, and level of communication needed at a certain time will help you better address both of your needs. It will also lead you to a feeling and reality of peace and understanding with each other. This is the goal that God has for us in our relationships, and it comes again from laying aside our needs to focus on the needs of others. As the message of the song says, seek first to understand before trying to be understood. God also says it to us in many ways. In James 1:19–20, "Everyone should be quick to listen, slow to speak and slow to become anger, for man's anger does not bring about the righteous life that God desires." In 1 Corinthians 13:4, "Love is patient, love is kind." In Ephesians 4:3, "Make every effort to keep the unity of the Spirit through the bond of peace." And in Hebrews 12:27, "Make every effort to live in peace with all men and to be holy; without holiness no one will see the Lord."

God wants us to be happy and fulfilled in our marriages. He wants us to enjoy our cruise. He wants us to know that by meeting the needs of our husband or wife, we will be living in patience and peace, and therefore we are much more able to enjoy our journey.

Chapter 3
Reflection Activity:
Improving Communication

1. List ways that you can enhance communication with your spouse. Discuss these ways with your spouse to see if they are in agreement that they will be effective.

2. Determine your love language and have your spouse determine his or her love language. List ways that you can communicate love to your spouse in ways they would appreciate.

3. Prayer:

   Lord, you have called us to love each other above all else. Even though we may feel this love for each other, we may not always be communicating it or expressing it through actions. Help us to realize when to speak, when to listen, and when to act. Give us patient ears and thoughtful words with our spouse so that they may know the way we truly feel. In Jesus's name we pray. Amen.

Couple Time

In this same way husbands ought to love their wives as their own bodies. He who loves his wife loves himself. After all, no one ever hated his own body, but he feeds and cares for it, just as Christ does the church—for we are members of His body.

Ephesians 5:28–30

The large cruise lines have learned that even though you are on board with hundreds of other people when sailing, they need to provide customers with a feeling of seclusion and opportunities for couples to feel romantic. If the cruise lines recognize the need for *couple time*, why don't we? We need time to renew our relationship and to remember why we decided to embark on this journey together in the first place!

Living in Green Bay, Wisconsin, brings exposure to the history of one of the greatest teams in the National Football League: the Green Bay Packers. Acclaimed coach Vince Lombardi is known for being determined, focused, and expecting a lot out of his players. He and his teams won two Super Bowls and grew to legendary status. The Super Bowl Trophy, the Lombardi Trophy, is named after him. Vince Lombardi knew how to achieve greatness, but he also knew that the job he did at work did not come first. Vince Lombardi prioritized life as "God, family, the team." He knew that he needed to have his life in order with God and at home before he could focus on what was happening on the field.

God, however, wants us to be more specific than Lombardi. He wants us to focus on God, spouse, family, the team. He should always come first, and we'll look at this as the sixth *C*—*C*hrist-centered. Right now, let's focus on what needs to come next. When you first fall in love, romance and intimacy with your spouse comes easily. As the relationship ages, other things take ownership of our time—work, children, commitments outside the home, responsibilities, church, etc. We often feel pulled in a million directions and are utterly exhausted when we finally have time to talk to our spouse. But God wants us to realize that if our marriage is not strong, the foundation of the entire family is not strong.

The fourth *C* as you sail the seven *C*s of marriage is *couple time*. Couple time includes the idea of the quality as well as quantity of time. Making time to stay close to your spouse and remain intimate is crucial in keeping your marriage as strong as it can be. A friend thought this *C* should be *consummation*. (Yes, the friend is a man.) However, intimacy is much more than sex. Sex will be the culmination of the relationship that you and your spouse have built, and yes, it is an important piece of the puzzle.

But forgetting the other pieces involved in building the relationship will leave your puzzle incomplete and lacking the big picture.

Before delving into the idea of couple time and intimacy, let's consider the gender issue again. Many men are made to crave physical intimacy with their wives, and many women are made to crave mental intimacy or relational closeness. Mark Gungor states in his video series Laugh Your Way to a Better Marriage that about 90 percent of each gender fit the stereotype associated with it. If this is not true for you, please do not think you are not normal. As Gungor jokingly puts it, if as a husband you have a wife that is usually more interested in sex than you are, the other 90 percent of the men in the room hate you! (He says this with a smile.) So if the roles are reversed for you, as with many I know, no problem.

I just explained that quality and quantity time need to precede intimacy. Let's first, however, look at why God created us with passion and the desire for intimacy and told us we should marry if we cannot control that desire. In the Bible, God has a definite goal in mind for marital intimacy. In our intimacy we are brought closer together as the one body we have become. Just as marriage is the highest form of love, sex within marriage is the highest form of expressing that love. As the couple grows closer and closer over time, the act of sex grows more and more fulfilling as well. Building a bond this strong allows the couple to be united at all times, not just during the intimate moments. It then becomes easier to consider the other's thoughts and feelings. The Bible tells us this.

> But at the beginning of creation God made them male and female. For this reason a man will leave his father and mother and be united to his wife, and the two will become one flesh. So they are no longer two, but one.
>
> Mark 10:6–8 (NIV)

> The husband should fulfill his marital duty to his wife, and likewise the wife to her husband. The wife's body does not belong to her alone but also to her husband. In the same way, the husband's body does not belong to him alone but also to his wife. Do not deprive each other except by mutual consent and for a time, so that you may devote yourselves to prayer. Then come together again so that Satan will not tempt you because of your lack of self-control.
>
> 1 Corinthians 7:3–6 (NIV)

Sex is an intensely physical act of the joining of husband and wife. It symbolizes a very deep union and brings with it intense emotions that become heightened over time. In their book *The Spark*, Jay and Laura Laffoon refer to the desired intimacy in marriage as holy sex. They define it as being one intellectually, emotionally, socially, and physically and that your blended interests and experiences lead you to a deeper sense of intimacy (Laffoon, p. 32). Use the visual image of a rope with two separate strands. The strands remain individual, but they are physically touching in many areas. When they are intertwined, they become stronger. When you become intertwined with your spouse, it strengthens your marriage.

You cannot become intertwined with your spouse unless you choose to. Having a headache or being too tired does not lead to intimacy. Making your spouse feel guilty for not being intimate does not bring the two of you closer. The goal is to get to the place where love is being freely given, not purchased or threatened. This is difficult for many women if the romance leading up to sex is not present. Without that essential piece, a woman may feel that her body is all her mate cherishes, which leads her to feel like a prostitute.

King Solomon knew about the art of romance and how to make his wife feel special in giving of herself. In Song of Songs 8:7, Solomon says, "Many waters cannot quench love; rivers cannot wash it away." He freely expressed his love to her, which enabled her to reciprocate as in Song of Songs 7:10: "I belong to my lover, and his desire is for me." God is the author of human love. This book, written by Solomon and inspired by God, is different than any other book in the Bible with its free language and expression. God gives us the book of Song of Songs so that we may read and remember what true passion for our spouse is.

To be able to speak as Solomon does to his wife requires trust of and devotion to the other person. Some scholars say this book is a true picture of how Christ loves His church— freely, passionately, and undeniably. Since marriage is the highest form of love we as humans can express and it is modeled after Christ's love for us, we find comfort, not discomfort or embarrassment, in the outward expression of emotion.

> My lover is mine and I am his; he browses among the lilies. Until the day breaks and the shadows flee, turn, my lover, and be like a gazelle or like a young stag on the rugged hills.
>
> Song of Songs 2:16–17 (NIV)

> I have come into my garden, my sister, my bride; I have gathered my myrrh with my spice. I have eaten my honeycomb and my honey; I have drunk my wine and my milk.
>
> Song of Songs 5:1 (NIV)

True love is secure. Imagine the greatest love of all, Jesus's love for us. Romans chapter 12:9 states that "love must be sincere." God does not want us to have to fake this important part of togetherness. He wants us to truly focus and enjoy one another so that we may experience the love He had intended for us.

Unfortunately, our society today has the meaning of sex all wrong. Movies, TV shows, the Internet, etc., offer sex as self-gratification, using someone else for your physical pleasure. This shallow view of sex destroys the meaning of God's plan: giving yourself freely to the other person you have committed your life to as the ultimate expression of love. To portray intimacy as acceptable between two people attracted to each other, trying to meet a physical need outside of marriage makes it much more difficult for them to form a meaningful commitment later on. There is much research done on the devastating effects that sex outside of marriage has on both men and women. If you are raising children, I encourage you to get this research as they will learn about sexually transmitted diseases in school, but not about the mental and emotional toll it will take on them and their marriages.

It has become harder and harder to not be distracted by the physical nature of sex in our society, but it has become more important to do so. Children and teens do not have many healthy role models in the area of marriage and sex in the media. We must capture for them on a daily basis what God intended for marriage so that they too can understand and strive to experience the wonderful plan God has in store for them.

In this book of the Bible, we also see that there are friends having dialogue with the lover and his beloved. They are supporting the couple's love and rejoicing in it.

They model the fact that we need to be supportive of each other's marriages and not try to weaken them. "We rejoice and delight in you, we will praise your love more than wine" (Song of Songs 1:4).

If a husband and wife are secure in their love and their relationship, they do not have to try to win each other over in public. If they are not secure, a woman may try to dress provocatively to show her husband that she can still get the attention of other men, or a man may flirt with other women in order to show his wife he is still desirable. When we do this, we weaken not only our own marriages but those of our friends and neighbors. God wants us to be supportive of each other. To do this well, it is important that we feel secure in our own marriages. It is difficult in today's society when so many of us are not secure in ourselves.

Self-esteem is an issue for many people. I have a friend who constantly says things like "I don't know why my husband is with me" or "I'm still shocked that he loves me." She puts herself down to the point of belittling herself and putting him on a pedestal. Sure, he's a great guy, but she is equally deserving of being classified as a great girl! Until we realize this in ourselves, it is difficult to contribute to that security in your relationship. But unless you become comfortable that you are a worthy and an equal partner, you will weaken even the most selfless spouse that can grow tired of trying to build you up all of the time.

We all struggle with different issues such as body image, being shy or introverted, perceived intelligence, perceived lack of power, any number of things that can diminish the picture of ourselves based on society's standards. God does not make mistakes. I remind myself of this whenever I encounter a person I am not connecting with or comfortable with, but I often forget to apply this thinking to myself. I forget to love the person God made me to be as much as He loves me. We forget that we are created in the image of God and that we are to treat ourselves as such. As Psalm 139:14 says, "I will praise you because I am fearfully and wonderfully made; your works are wonderful, I know that full well."

In being comfortable with ourselves as precious creations, we are more comfortable to give of ourselves in the marriage relationship. As this giving needs to be selfless and focused on our spouse, we are more able to do that when we are not focused on our own inadequacies. It is easier to enter into intimacy with our spouse if deep in our minds we know we are doing so out of true love and commitment and not just to make up for something we feel we are lacking. Intimacy is a crucial part of marriage. Let's take a look at what needs to lead to marital intimacy and how it will grow more and more fulfilling over time.

Much to the dismay of many men, most women can't just turn on the intimacy switch or go to the sex box in their brain. It's not that easy. For most women and some men, sex is the culmination of time and experiences shared. It is knowing that your spouse appreciates you. It is having love communicated in your language. For most men, sex is a physical desire they yearn to have satisfied. A friend once told me that if you are not meeting the desires of your husband, there are many women out there who will!

The most important thing to remember in marriage is love must be *selfless* and that we are to do what is in the best interest of the other person *because* we love them. Being human, this is something we must strive for as being selfish comes much more easily to us than being selfless. We need to meet the needs of our spouse for that reason, but there are fringe benefits to our acts of service. Our spouse will be much more willing to meet our needs as well!

Think of your first date. Was it anything spectacular or awesome? Or was it great just because it was your first date? When first attracted to your spouse, romantic feelings came very easily. We thought about our spouse constantly, and the figurative butterflies arose in our stomach at the mere mention of his name. We desired to be near him, and we couldn't spend enough time with him. Fast-forward.

Now, many things get in the way of spending quality and quantity time with our spouse. They may have fallen from priority number 1 to not even making the list at all. Life has become so busy that we lose sight of our ultimate goal: living the life we were created for, following the plan God laid out for us, and spreading His Word through serving others. We forget the priority list as suggested by

Lombardi: God, family, team. We let "team" (whatever that may be in our lives) sometimes come before family and before God. We need to stop and look at our calendars. Have we scheduled time for God? Have we scheduled time for our family? Have we scheduled time alone with our spouse? Our time is one of the greatest resources we have. We need to spend it wisely.

The quality and quantity of time with our spouse is, for many, that vital bridge to intimacy. Consider this scenario asserted by Jay and Laura Laffoon. Most men physically desire sex every seventy-two hours on average. For them, *when all is all right in the bedroom, all is all right with the world.* Sex empowers them and gives them the confidence that their marriage is secure, and when that is the case, they are more secure with themselves. For most women, however, for them to be in the mood for sex, they need to be wooed, understood, and valued. *When all is all right with the world, all is all right in the bedroom.* The Laffoons offer a picture to help us see this relationship.

Intercourse

Intimacy culminates for most women

Intimacy begins for most men

Remembering that our relationship mirrors that of Jesus and the church, Jesus (representing the husband) is the pursuer, and the church (representing the wife) is the pursued. We take great comfort and are left in awe that Jesus wants us to follow Him at all costs and loves us enough to give up His life for us. A woman craves this desire for her from her husband and needs to know regularly that he cherishes and wants her. In the same regard, Jesus seeks commitment and respect for the Father from His church and a commitment to follow Him. A husband craves this respect from his wife, and when it is offered freely, he is stronger for it.

Knowing that time and the little things that we do each day to prioritize our spouse build to intimacy, we strive to find ways to communicate love to our spouse and to schedule in time for him or her. You may have seen the activity with the glass jar. The speaker will fill the jar with rocks and ask if it's full. It looks full, but then he takes sand and pours sand over the rocks. There was room. Now is it full? He then takes water and is able to add water to the jar. This activity is meant to illustrate that you can fit a lot into that jar, and that jar represents the time in your schedule. The rocks represent the priorities in your life. The time with your spouse is one of those important rocks. If you start filling your schedule with sand and water first, the rocks will not fit. You need to begin scheduling your time with the important things and then filling in around them. As the most important rock in our jar, our marriage relationships deserve check-in time daily, dates frequently, and memorable times annually.

Realistically, every night cannot be date night, but there should be a time each day for you to connect with each other without interruption. This check-in time could be anywhere from ten to thirty minutes and may be on the phone, may be after children are in bed, or may be at the table after dinner is done. We share so much time and information with others on a daily basis that we need to share as well with our spouse. Remembering Gary Chapman's levels of communication, this time may afford us the opportunity to only get to level 2 (reporter) or 3 (intellectual) conversation, but that is probably what we have shared with others throughout the day and what our spouse deserves from us as well.

Dates are confined only by your interests as a couple and your imagination. Each spouse may have a different idea of what a great date could be. Honoring your spouse's interests shows greater love, support, and commitment. The standby dinner and a movie may be of high interest to some couples, but don't rule out a long walk with our without a destination, a sporting event, a shopping afternoon, a musical performance, an art show, a drive in the country, or an afternoon picnic. You may have been drawn to some suggestions and not others. Your spouse could be drawn to different suggestions. Honoring and appreciating our differences helps us grow closer as a couple. Notice that this short list includes activities that come with a cost and activities that are free. Dates don't need to be expensive to be meaningful.

"Memorable times need to be intentionally planned for. I suggest a memorable time needs to be an extended period of time (at least a weekend) away from distractions and occur at least on an annual basis. I have a plaque in my house surrounded by pictures of our family that says "Life is not measured by the breaths you take but by the moments that take your breath away." That saying reminds me that my husband and children won't remember particular dates of special events or vacations but that we will remember the sights, smells, and sensations that we felt during special times together.

I find myself relishing those memories and having them remind me of how important our relationships are. To have those special memories between you and your spouse helps you see them more often as that invaluable person in your life. Those special times that you can look forward to and look back on act like glue that help to strengthen your bond as husband and wife. These events can be special vacations and getaways on a large scale or small scale but should center around time meant for just the two of you. Get as elaborate as a trip to Tuscany or as simple as a camping trip to the next county; either way, you'll be making memorable moments together.

Couple time requires the intentional planning of quantity and quality time. Spending time together helps solidify your bond as one and leads to a more fulfilling and intimate relationship. Making sure your spouse's needs are met can be the most rewarding part of spending couple time together!

Chapter 4
Reflection Activity:
Planning Meaningful Couple Time

1. Make a list of at least five up to as many as you want of things you can do in each of the three categories of check-ins, dates, and memorable times.

2. Put two of your dates on the calendar. Let your spouse pick something they would like to do together for one, and you should pick something you would like to do together for the other one. Follow through with those dates!

3. Prayer:

Loving God, You always have time for us and love us unconditionally and sincerely. As you desire us to spend more time alone with you, may we also desire to spend more time alone with our spouse. May we harness the love that we feel for our spouse and make time to spend with them. May this time produce a deeper love for each other as we discover and rediscover the qualities you gave to our spouse and appreciate them even more. May our time together be fun, fantastic, and fruitful. In Jesus's name we pray. Amen.

Currency

Choose my instruction instead of silver, knowledge rather than choice gold, for wisdom is more precious than rubies, and nothing you desire can compare with her.

—Proverbs 8:10–11

So far we have been looking at building a strong sea-worthy vessel in our marriage that can take on any rough waters. Many of us promise to be committed to each other "in sickness and in health, for richer and for poorer." According to *Money Magazine*, negotiating the richer or poorer part is a huge storm that severely damages or sinks many strong marriages. In a survey of one thousand spouses, respondents reported that they argue more about money than about sex and that 84 percent said money causes tension in their marriages. *Currency* is a topic that needs to be discussed with purpose so that it does not capsize our marriage vessel.

In an article entitled "The Six Financial Mistakes Couples Make," Aleksandra Todorova states "Numerous studies have shown that money is the No. 1 reason why couples argue—and many of the recently divorced say those battles were the main reason why they untied the knot" *(Family Money,* June 11, 2008). Couples argue about spending, saving, investing, and prioritizing. We may have very different ideas as husband and wife about what to do with our money. Realizing that we may be different in our approach is the first step to coming up with a plan together.

Jesus knew that managing our money would be difficult. He wants us to remember that the money we make or that is given to us is not ours but God's. It is up to us to be responsible stewards of that money and do with it what God asks us to do. He warns us not to become obsessed with that which is not ours. "As a result, he does not live the rest of his earthly life for evil human desires, but rather for the will of God" (1 Peter 4:2).

> But godliness with contentment is great gain. For we brought nothing into the world, and we can take nothing out of it. But if we have food and clothing, we will be content with that. People who want to get rich fall into temptation and a trap and into many foolish and harmful desires that plunge men into ruin and destruction. For the love of money is a root of all kinds of evil.
>
> 1 Timothy 6:6–10 (NIV)

> I tell you the truth, it is hard for a rich man to enter the kingdom of heaven. Again I tell you, it is easier for a camel to go through the eye of a needle than for a rich man to enter the kingdom of God.
>
> Matthew 19:23 (NIV)

If the money that we have been entrusted with is from God, we need to know what He wants us to do with it in order to adhere to His plan. We are given the following principles to follow so that we can be not only smart with God's money as a couple but also obedient. He wants us to remember that financial security is a blessing. Consider the acronym of BLESS to capture the steps we should take: *blend* our money, *lay* out a plan, *enter* evidence, *share* opinions, *serve* others.

Blend Our Money

When we enter marriage, we are uniting as one body. We cannot become one marriage unit with separate finances. Couples need to have this discussion before the wedding so that there are no surprises. My husband, Steve, is an accountant. This step was an important one for him prior to marriage. He asked me for a full financial disclosure when our relationship got to that point. I have to admit, when he asked me for this disclosure, at first I felt a little violated. I was teaching at the college level and substitute teaching in about ten different area school districts. I had a bachelor and master's degree and a little bit of school debt. Is that really his business? Well, okay, yes it was because if we were to be joined together, he had a right to know my income, debt, spending habits, and philosophy. It's all there in black-and-white, and he'll find out anyway. *Hopefully*, I thought, *it won't make him love me any less*. Of course it didn't. He just needed to know what our finances would look like once joined.

With blended finances, all income is pooled, and there is no "mine" or "yours." Instead there is "ours." It doesn't matter who makes more, whether one spouse is not working, or what debt one or both may bring to the relationship. Approaching our financial life with the attitude that what we each bring becomes what we each own is important to honor our *commitment* to each other as a united couple. In most marriages, one partner has the responsibility of managing the overall financial picture, which we will discuss further, but their attitude must be as a manager of the provisions of both and not just one. "For this reason a man will leave his father and mother and be united to his wife, and they will become one flesh" (Genesis 2:24).

"Two are better than one, because they have a good return for their work" (Ecclesiastes 4:9).

Lay Out a Plan

Like any well-thought-out itinerary for a journey, there is a purpose and a plan. Many couples have never deeply addressed the issue of money. That is not to say they don't consult each other on large purchases or discuss whether or not they have money to take a vacation, but they really don't have long-term goals or a common understanding of each other's thoughts and dreams. This becomes a problem when we sail into unexpected storms. Although we can't foresee everything that will come our way in our life together, God tells us to be thoughtful in our approach. Proverbs 14:15 states, "A simple man believes anything, but a prudent man gives thought to his steps," and Proverbs 24:3 asserts, "By wisdom a house is built, and through understanding it is established."

> Suppose one of you wants to build a tower. Will he not first sit down and estimate the cost to see if he has enough money to complete it? For if he lays the foundation and is not able to finish it, everyone who sees it will ridicule him, saying, "This fellow began to build and was not able to finish."
>
> Luke 14:28–29 (NIV)

First and foremost in our plan is giving back to God a portion of what He has entrusted us. We know this as tithing. *Tithe* literally means "ten." We are instructed that this means giving one-tenth of what we have to the church. You can debate whether this is net income or gross income, but what it comes down to is truly 10 percent of what you bring in. We must be willing to again see that we have been blessed by God with our assets, and He is trusting that we will use them as we are told. We read in Leviticus 27:30, "A tithe of everything from the land, whether grain from the soil or fruit from the trees, belongs to the Lord; it is holy to the Lord."

God promises that if we follow the instruction of tithing, we will be blessed even further and trusted with even more of His riches on earth to deploy. I can definitely attest that we have never had more coming into our accounts than when we stick to giving 10 percent back to the church. Following these instructions reaps the reward because we are trusted. God tells us this in Malachi:

> I the Lord do not change. So you, O descendants of Jacob, are not destroyed. Ever since the time of your forefathers you have turned away from my decrees and have not kept them. Return to me, and I will return to you," says the Lord Almighty. But you ask "How are we to return?" Will a man rob God? Yet you rob me. But you ask, "How do we rob you? In tithes and offerings. You are under a curse—the whole nation of you—because you are robbing me. Bring the whole tithe into the storehouse, that there may be food in my house. "Test me in this," says the Lord Almighty, "and see if I will not throw open the floodgates of heaven and pour out so much blessing that you will not have room enough for it."

> Malachi 3:6–10 (NIV)

God wants us to trust Him with all our hearts and to prove this by giving Him His portion willingly and gratefully. Doing this proves to God that you are obedient and trust He will provide for you no matter what comes your way. It amazes me how God works through this promise if you let Him. I have heard countless stories of my friends receiving checks in the mail they did not know were coming for almost the exact dollar amount of an unforeseen expense. Things like that have happened to us on more than one occasion. It even makes me smile when I find $5 in the pocket of a coat that I forgot was there, and then a half an hour later one of my kids says they need $5 for something at school. I just grin and look up and say a prayer of thanksgiving, thinking, *You've done it again!*

Once you determine the 10 percent of all of your finances and put that willingly aside for God, you need to prioritize the rest of what you have been blessed with. You also need to know what your priorities, once established, mean on a weekly, monthly, and yearly basis. The questions you need to ask yourselves include, but are not limited to, the following when determining your plan:

- What kind of house do you need in order to be comfortable but yet able to not overburden your budget?

- What kind of car will get you from point A to point B and everything in between?

- What monthly bills are necessary to take care of?

- What portion of your income should go to clothes and food?

- ❖ How much do you give to charitable organizations after church?
- ❖ How much do you need to save for retirement or your children's college fund?

Both partners need to have equal input in the plan. When we discuss sharing our opinions, you'll see that you and your spouse can have very different outlooks on what to do with your money, and neither one is necessarily good or bad, right or wrong. Considering each other's priorities and goals, and again listening selflessly, will help establish a plan that both of you can commit to wholeheartedly. Going through life with your mate without a financial plan is like sailing through the seven *C*s without an itinerary, drifting aimlessly without an end in mind. One spouse may want to sail one way and the other in the opposite direction. Without financial plans or goals, you may find yourself years later without enough for important opportunities that come your way or your children's way. You may look back regretting that you can't do something one or both of you truly looked forward to.

Enter Evidence

Depending on our strengths, it is fine for either spouse to be in charge of the record keeping and probably easier if it is just one. Ultimately, however, the husband is accountable for the family and for the final decisions.

> He must manage his own family well and see that
> his children obey him with proper respect. If anyone
> does not know how to manage his own family, how
> can he take care of God's church?
>
> 1 Timothy 3:4–5 (NIV)

As you know, my husband is an accountant. There was a time early on in our marriage when I really wanted to have an understanding of all of the money that came in and went out of our accounts on a monthly basis. I asked Steve to let me do the books for a few months in order to gain this insight. Begrudgingly, he handed over the reins. After a few weeks of me paying the bills as soon as they came, Steve pleaded with me to take back the task. I later learned that there are key times of the month to pay each bill and that I was screwing up his system. I gladly gave back control as he honestly enjoys doing it much more than me. We have, however, come to the understanding that I need an update in this area twice a year to make sure I understand and have input in the process.

It is extremely important to know what you bring in financially as well as what you expend. Once you have set a plan for your finances, you need to stick to it and be able to prove whether or not the plan is working. Think of it as a diet. No matter what your goal—to lose weight, to gain muscle, etc.—you need to know if what you are doing is working. You need to keep track of the amount of calories and what kind of calories are coming into your body, and you need to know how much energy you are expending on a daily basis. Understanding this balance helps you know whether or not your action plan is effective and keeping you on track. It helps you understand whether or not you are sticking to your diet!

Once you've laid out your financial plan, you need to know if both of you are following it by keeping track of your expenditures. This requires open and honest communication. We can't hide this vital information from our spouse. We need to practice full disclosure. Having said that, it upset me every time I wanted to buy Steve a gift. If I didn't pay cash for a purchase, Steve could look in the checkbook or at the credit card statement and make an educated guess based on the store and the amount what he was about to receive. As an accountant, and a very good one at that, he has instant messages coming to him every time our credit card is used so that he can be notified if something ever goes wrong. One time my girlfriend and I took full advantage of this fact by having a special day together and allowing Steve to be in on our every purchase by credit card: a cup of coffee here, a truffle at the chocolate shop there, etc. I don't think he found it very funny.

Steve and I finally came to the agreement that I needed a credit card in a separate account that he agreed not to check. My side of the agreement is that I am only to use it for gifts for him and nothing else and not to go overboard. This agreement honors the fact that he trusts me and allows me to have my "element of surprise" yet gives him the ability to open the statement and reconcile the finances when I give him the green light to do so. I have to also trust that he wouldn't peek! So far, so good.

Share Opinions

We know how each of us is different in many ways, and that is evident also in the way we approach our finances. Understanding that your approach and your spouse's approach are different helps you to value his or her perspective. In their book *First Comes Love, Then Comes Money*, Scott and Bethany Palmer classify our differences into money styles and assert that each of us have two of the five styles, one being primary and the other being secondary. The five styles include being a saver, spender, security seeker, risk taker, or a flyer. There are pros and cons to each style, but being aware of your style as well as your spouse's will help you come to consensus when developing and sticking to your plan.

One of you may be a saver and be very thrifty with your money, spending only when you have to and often consciously going without. The positive aspects of this money style are that you don't rely on the newest fads, need stuff in order to be happy, or spend frivolously. The negatives may include waiting too long to buy something that is needed or worrying about having enough saved and not trusting in God to provide.

On the other hand, you may be a spender. Whether you enjoy a great deal and thrive on coupons or if you never look at the price tag, you spend money quite easily and can conjure up any logic needed to defend your purchases. The positive side to spenders is that they are often very generous and want to buy for others, sometimes even more than they want to buy for themselves. Of course, a negative is that the money going out of the household may end up being more than the money coming in or more than they thought after recording their purchases.

The security seeker is one who will rarely take chances with their money. In no way does buying a lottery ticket seem like a good investment. This person never quite feels like he will have enough for a rainy day. More often than not, this person needs a plan and prioritizes saving. He will approach spending carefully and never wants to take a risk.

Then you have the risk takers. "You can't make money unless you spend money" may be their motto. They win big and may lose big. They may be fun to watch in a casino, providing adrenaline rushes to themselves and to those around them. The payoff may be worth it, but the result may also be devastating.

Finally there is the flyer. This person does not worry about money much at all. It is not a source of stress, but oftentimes it is not something they truly understand either. There may be a carefree attitude toward money, or there may be a severe lack of knowledge about finances and economy in general.

Again, the Palmers say we each embody two of the five styles with one being a little more dominant than the other. I would think it rare to be in a marriage with someone who has your exact combination. Assuming that there are differences in your styles and your approach to the money we have established as shared, it is easy to see why this area can cause couples a great deal of tension and stress. Being aware of and understanding your spouse's money style will help you appreciate his or her opinion when making a financial decision. There is no right way, so one spouse should not always dominate. Honoring each other's styles on the little decisions helps one partner or the other accept the point of view that makes the most sense on the bigger decision.

Serve Others

When prioritizing your budget after tithing, it is essential to plan around a stable household where your family's basic needs are met. Shelter, food, clothing, health care, and saving for the future of you and your spouse, as well as for possible opportunities for your children, are all crucial things to consider. After that, I believe God wants us to enjoy life and enjoy the fruits of our labor like any loving father would. But He also commands us to share with those less fortunate than ourselves.

> Command those who are rich in this present world
> not to be arrogant nor to put their hope in wealth,
> which is so uncertain, but to put everything for our
> enjoyment. Command them to do good, to be rich
> in good deeds, and to be generous and willing to
> share.
>
> 1 Timothy 6:27 (NIV)

We are commanded to be willing to help out others in need.
We can be generous in our good deeds, with our time, or
with our money. By being generous to others, we are again
providing a role model of how God commands us to live.
If we account for everything we give and make the receiver
feel indebted to us, we are not examples of Christ's love.
We make others wonder why we, as Christians, promote
selflessness but are not able to practice what we preach. We
need to give with an open heart.

I bring this aspect of finances up as you and your spouse
may have different ideas of how you want to display this
generosity. Unless money is not an issue for you at all and
you have more than you will ever need, this is an area that
you and your spouse need to consider. I work at a school
with a very high poverty rate. Need is all around me, but I
can't give money to every student or parent in need every
day. If there are big issues, I will contact my husband and
ask his opinion, and we'll come to an agreement on what
we should do. With small needs like a bus pass or a lunch,
I will make that determination on my own. If Steve wants

to donate to an organization in memory of his father, we discuss and budget for that. If I want to donate to an organization that supports me in my faith, I let him know so that we can decide on an amount together.

We are also commanded directly to look after two distinct groups of people.

> Religion that God our Father accepts as pure and faultless is this: to look after orphans and widows in their distress and to keep oneself from being polluted by the world.
>
> James 1:27 (NIV)

When Steve and I lived in our first house, there was a widow who lived next door to us named Edna. The first day that Steve moved in (he bought the house before we were married), Edna came over with a bag of cucumbers, and he knew instantly that he had picked the right house. Ever since that day, we had a special bond with Edna and remained close to her even after moving twenty miles away. Our boys knew her as Great-Grandma by Proxy, and we visited her often. We took care of her in many ways, but she also took care of us. As an accountant, Steve did her taxes for over sixteen years, and as payment, he received an apple pie—with extra cinnamon. When it came to providing for Edna, generosity didn't seem like giving; it just seemed like a natural thing to do. We also sponsor a child in Africa named Ira. He is right in the middle of my son's ages, so he seems like a natural part of our family. Many families open their homes to orphans or children in need through foster care or adoption and find that even though it may be a struggle, their lives are richer in so many ways. My hope is that every one of us opens our heart to an "Edna" or an "Ira" as our life will be better for it.

Financial issues can be the cause of great stress in marriage, but they don't have to be. By understanding our spouse's approach to money as well as his or her financial goals, we can alleviate both misunderstandings and budget nightmares. *Blending* your money, *laying* out a plan, *entering* evidence, *sharing* your opinions, and remembering to *serve* others will allow God to further BLESS your marriage and entrust you with more to share.

Chapter 5
Reflection Activity:
Current Currency

You will need to set aside time for this activity, and it may require you to reflect separately as well as together if you've never deeply discussed the area of *currency* in your marriage.

1. Identify your primary and your secondary money type.

2. Reflect on your short-term and long-term financial goals.

3. Share these money types and financial goals with your partner.

4. If you don't have a budget, this is a biggie. Go back to the section on "laying out a plan" and establish the items you need to address in your financial plan. Know your total income and expenditures, and see if your habits are matching your priorities and financial goals.

5. Make a commitment to periodically and honestly review your financial plan.

6. Prayer:

Lord, We know that all of the gifts we obtain on earth are gifts from above. You entrust us to make wise decisions yet be selfless with our possessions. Help us to trust that you will provide and care for us, but realize that we must also take responsibility for Your kingdom as best we can. In Jesus's name we pray, amen.

Christin-Centered

We have this hope as an anchor for the soul, firm
and secure.

Hebrews 6:19

Sailing through life on a beautiful journey is impossible to
fathom without an anchor. If we are not able to be anchored
in His word, we will drift aimlessly, pulled by the currents
and rocked by the waves. The most important *C* (or double
C) of the seven is *C*hrist-centered. You may wonder why,
if it is the most important chapter, is it sixth? Let me
explain. Your marriage should begin Christ-centered.
Before marriage, it is important that you and your spouse
are Christ-centered as individuals. Many people, many
Christians, know this in theory but really don't know what
it means to live life as Christ-centered individuals. Many
of us are SOCs (Sunday Only Christians). We do not have
that personal relationship with our Lord and Savior, which
makes it difficult to understand the plan He has for us in
our lives. Not that the other five *C*s are easy by any means,
but this one may take the most introspection. I first wanted
to discuss the meaning of marriage and how to build a solid
foundation within the home before leading the discussion
directly to God. Although He is the most critical element

in a successful and fulfilling marriage, to some He is also the most elusive. We also needed to understand the concepts of communication and couple time because being Christ-centered in your marriage is so reliant on these two.

Many couples believe that by working on their marriage alone, just the two of them, they will find fulfillment. They forget that they need two crucial elements before embarking on their journey: an itinerary or guidebook and an anchor. Only God can provide these items. If we are not Christ-centered, we become world-centered. We let our marriages be influenced by society, the media, the entertainment industry, the fashion industry, and others. If we are not careful, this can lead to others dictating our worth as individuals and our roles as husband or wife within our marriage. If we let society determine our worth or the worth of our marriage, we allow ourselves to be marginalized, and we become casualties of the world like so many others. The world has a dangerous current. We need Christ at the center of our lives as an anchor against the current. If our marriage is to be successful as defined by the Creator of marriage, we must remain centered on His word.

> If you belonged to the world, it would love you as its own. As it is, you do not belong to the world, but I have chosen you out of the world. That is why the world hates you. I have told you these things, so that in me you may have peace. In this world you

will have trouble. But take heart! I have overcome
the world.

John 15:19, 16:33 (NIV)

We also have high expectations that our spouse will
meet all of our hopes and dreams. We forget that we are
human and sinful by nature. Only when we look to Christ
as our Savior from sin as well as our support within our
relationships and all that we do will we be truly successful.
No other person can fulfill the deep needs within us, and
no other person accepts us unconditionally 100 percent of
the time.

We talked previously in communication about it taking
a lot of trust to get to the deep levels of loving/truth talk
to be able to share our thoughts and feelings. Prayer is
the culmination of sharing your hopes, dreams, fears, and
praise. Many find it safe to pray in church with others
around us reading in unison. It is also easy to pray silently
to God by ourselves. It is a little more difficult to be part of
or lead prayer for a small group or off the cuff at the dinner
table. But it is much harder to get to the level of trust in
communication to pray one-on-one with our spouse. This
is the person that knows us the best. This is the person who
we so want to see the good in us. But this is also the person
who needs to be part of the equation when building that
solid foundation in a marriage. Put simply, the couple that
prays together *stays* together!

"The process of becoming one spiritually occurs when a husband and wife mutually commit to being conformed to the image of Christ" (Laffoon, p. 113). Christ has to be at the center of our marriage as no one human is perfect and can meet all of the expectations and desires we have but Him. Think of your marriage as a team effort. You and your spouse are the athletes, but God is the coach. Without Him, you may have great rapport and camaraderie, but lack direction. We interact on a daily basis with each other, but we must also interact together with Christ to keep us focused.

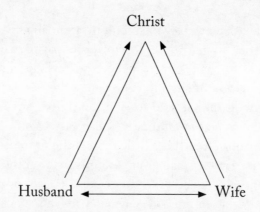

The Bible says we are not to be alone with our prayers but together as we strive to walk in the Word of God. "Submit to one another out of reverence for Christ" (Ephesians 5:21).

"He who conceals his sins does not prosper, but whoever confesses and renounces them finds mercy" (Proverbs 28:13).

"Therefore confess your sins to each other and pray for each other so that you may be healed. The prayer of a righteous man is powerful and effective" (James 5:16).

> Be very careful, then, how you live—not as unwise but as wise, making the most of every opportunity, because the days are evil. Speak to one another with psalms, hymns and spiritual songs. Sing and make music in your heart to the Lord, always giving thanks to God the Father for everything in the name of our Lord Jesus Christ.
>
> Ephesians 5:15–16, 19 (NIV)

And most important is in Matthew 18:20: "For where two or three come together in my name, there am I with them."

Consider the term *spiritual intimacy*. What does that term mean to you? Some definitions may include "connecting to one another through Christ," "being on the same page as a couple with the Holy Spirit," "trusting and obeying God together, allowing Him to be in control," "praying together and respecting each other's input during prayer," and "serving, worshiping, and praying together." Think of spiritual intimacy as a rope.

In *couple time*, we looked at how each spouse needs to be intertwined with their partner as if braiding two separate pieces of rope together. Two strands intertwined are stronger than one, but still do not make a very strong rope. When you add that third strand, you increase its strength exponentially. Adding Christ to our husband-and-wife relationship makes it that much stronger. Whatever your definition of spiritual intimacy, for many couples, spiritual intimacy is the hardest to come by.

Spiritual intimacy requires letting down walls and ultimately putting your trust as a couple not just in each other, but in Christ. It is easier to do this with a stranger than with another who knows all of your innermost secrets. "Prayer is probably one of the most vulnerable, intimate actions a couple can do together" (Laffoon, p. 121). When the walls come down, truth is revealed, and at that point, we can ultimately support each other.

An important piece of coming closer together and being Christ-centered is not hiding things from one another, but confessing your thoughts, feelings, and sins. Then couples must ask for and grant forgiveness to each other in order to move forward in their relationship with each other and with God. Many people, when asked what is most important in a good marriage, will state the ability to forgive and to be forgiven. We looked at the importance of forgiveness when discussing our marriage as a commitment. Let's look at it again from the angle of modeling our marriage around Christ's commitment to His church.

I am amazed that Jesus forgives me over and over again. If our marriage is a reflection of Christ and the church, we need to practice forgiveness as well. This doesn't mean that we shouldn't be remorseful and apologetic. The crazy thing is that sometimes we don't even realize we wronged our spouse. This is when forgiveness and honest communication go hand in hand. I may not realize that saying something about Steve in a conversation with others hurt him. He may not realize that he discarded my opinion on an important issue and hurt me in the process. It is up to us to maturely share our hurt but, more importantly, forgive the other person and not harbor the hurt or the anger.

Wait a minute. Does that mean I'm to tell my husband when I spent above our budget or tell him what is hurting me when I think he should already know? Yes. Does that mean I need to tell my wife that I just need time alone or that I struggle with pornography? Yes. Does that mean that we need to come together regularly to confess to each other our struggles and fears and pray for strength? Yes. Wow... that's pretty scary stuff. Again, this is why I saved this *C* for later on in the discussion. It requires a deep commitment to each other regarding what is shared, the understanding of how to trust each other in our communication, and time prioritized for each other to be away from distractions and focus. Let me give you some suggestions for how to start this process.

Start first with the Word of God. Look for a Bible that has an index of topics. Start with some verses that are easier and move into some themes you may struggle with. Or buy a Christian book that has daily devotions for you to read together and then discuss. Steve and I received a book like this for our wedding called *Quiet Time for Couples*. Each day has a Bible verse and then a reflection of that verse that leads into discussion questions for couples. Topics such as fatigue, going astray, and even communication can be saved for daily couple time. Remember back to the couple ordering a conversation off a menu? Well, consider this the not-so-desperate version of that. We are making time for the Word of God and what it means to us both personally and as well as a couple. What a great way to express ourselves on a topic while remaining focused on the purpose.

Being *Christ-centered* as a couple is the most important *C* because in the end, all of the other *C*s fall directly from His Word. We have to humble ourselves and balance the control we have in our lives with the faith we must have in Him and our hope for eternity. He wants us to rely on Him because He loves us. He wants us to remember to love each other as Christ loved us. We are called to be imitators of Christ. What does that mean? It means we walk in love because God is love. Love is how we imitate Him, how we learn who we are and who our neighbor—in this case our spouse—is. Love is how we spiritually see and understand reality. We are called in everything to walk in love as the fulfillment of our basic calling and identity as children of the God who is love. Remember that God *commanded* us to love each other.

Reggie White, acclaimed Green Bay Packer defensive end, knew being Christ-centered was more important than anything else in life. An ordained minister and known as the Minister of Defense, Reggie led his teams in prayer regularly. He wanted his teammates and others to know how much God loves us. He reminded fans of this as often as he could by signing items brought to him, "Reggie White 92 1 Cor. 13." He knew that the only way to play the game of life was to have Christ on your side! "And now these three remain: faith, hope and love. But the greatest of these is love" (1 Corinthians 13:13).

Chapter 6
Reflection Activity:
Making God Central to Your Marriage

1. Write a brief prayer thanking God for your spouse.

2. Set a time to be alone together for about fifteen minutes. If you are comfortable praying together, read your prayer to your spouse. If you are not yet to that level of comfort, exchange prayers and read them silently.

3. Select a Bible passage or a daily devotional entry to read. Have a discussion as to the implications for you personally and as a couple.

4. Prayer:

    Heavenly Father, we are so thankful for the spouse you have given us to share our daily concerns and celebrations, our strengths and our weaknesses, our fears and our faith. Help us gain the comfort we need in each other to come closer to you *together*. We know that we need You at the center of our individual lives. Help us put You always at the center of our marriage. In Jesus's name we pray, amen.

Community

Whatever you do, work at it with all your heart as working for the Lord, not for men.

Colossians 3:23

Hopefully, you all had a honeymoon, and if not, I hope by now you are planning one. Think about that special time or think of a recent vacation. When on vacation, there is that moment, maybe many, when you just don't want the time to end. You want to stay away from "reality" and responsibility. Vacations and time away are important in order to recharge our batteries and to enjoy our spouse and our family if we choose to bring them along. But this special time does end, and we do need to come back to our purpose and our unique calling. We can't stay away from our work forever!

The last *C* we will discuss is *community*. I purposefully put it at the end. Building a strong marriage is what the first six chapters were about. Each component that you focus on, address, and then celebrate will help make your marriage grow stronger. But we are not meant to build a strong home and then stay secluded from others, only venturing out to replenish our food supply. Instead, we are made to serve others with the different gifts we have been given. In this chapter, we will look at how we can do God's will while we find strength from and give strength to our spouse in our endeavors. This occurs in three steps: establishing our *purpose*, determining the *impact* it will have on our home and family, and then building the *support* structure for each other to carry out our work.

Establishing Your Purpose

We are each uniquely and wonderfully made. We were given different gifts in order to fulfill the purpose God has planned for us. In marriage, it is crucial to remember that after God, our marriage and our family come first. After we have built that firm foundation by addressing the needs in the previous chapters, we must now support the work that God has given both ourselves and our spouse to do because that is ultimately why we were created. We all have work to do. Our work comes in many forms outside of the home. The essence of all of our work can be found in Mark 16:15 where we read, "He said to them, 'Go into all the world and preach the good news to all creation.'"

We are also shown the value of our work in the community many other places in the Bible. "Moreover, when God gives any man wealth and possessions and enables him to enjoy them, to accept his lot and be happy in his work—this is a gift of God" (Ecclesiastes 5:19).

"Do not merely listen to the word, and so deceive yourselves. Do what it says" (James 1:22).

"As long as it is day, we must do the work of him who sent me. Night is coming, when no one can work" (John 9:4).

"God is not unjust; he will not forget your work and the love you have shown him as you have helped his people and continue to help them" (Hebrews 6:10).

"There are different kinds of gifts but the same Spirit. There are different kinds of service, but the same Lord. There are different kinds of working, but the same God works all of them in all men" (1 Corinthians 12:4–6).

"We have different gifts according to the grace given us" (Romans 12:6).

Some of us have married a person with similar gifts and talents. Many of us, however, may have married a person who has been given far different gifts and talents than we have. The old theory of "opposites attract" is often at play. Whatever we are good at should be used to serve God, serve others, and expand His kingdom. Some of us were given the wisdom to lead, others the ability to teach, others the heart to serve, and still others the ability to heal. What a team we make with our spouse in service to God. "Now to each one the manifestation of the Spirit is given for the common good" (1 Corinthians 12:7).

This doesn't mean that we should all have a paying job outside of the home, volunteer for eight different nonprofit organizations, or leave the country for mission work. You may be called on to fulfill one of those scenarios, or you may not. Many women and men stay at home for good reasons, whether or not they have children. But they are called to fulfill their purpose by volunteering or serving others within the community with the gifts they have been given. I think of one friend who has never worked at a paying job, but she works daily for others by being there when a loved one is sick, bringing food to those in need, driving someone to an appointment, or volunteering where she is needed in the community. Quite frankly, she is so busy serving others she doesn't have time for a full-time job!

God calls it work because it does require time, attention, and energy. He wants us to put effort into what we do. We are not in this world to relax and take it easy, although God does tell us there is value in recharging our batteries and renewing our energy source to strengthen our commitment to what we are doing! He calls it work so that we may know we will have struggles along the way but that we should stick with it as we are working to serve God by serving others.

> Whatever you do, work at it with all your heart, as working for the Lord, not for men, since you know that you will receive an inheritance from the Lord as a reward. It is the Lord Christ you are serving.
>
> Colossians 3:23–24 (NIV)

Steve says I'm lucky. It is easy to make a difference in the work that I do. I do consider myself very fortunate to have served as a school administrator for almost two decades.

I am afforded many opportunities daily to serve others and be a role model for the Word of God. He says it is much more difficult to have an impact on others when you crunch numbers all day in an office. But I point out to him that he does have an impact on those he works with on a daily basis who may seek him out for advice or leadership. We are provided constant opportunities to do God's work in whatever setting we find ourselves. When you label yourself a Christian, you have constant responsibility to carry out the Word of God. Like many of you, Steve also makes a difference with his involvement in our church as well as with our boys' activities. Many people are drawn to coaching or leading a youth club or organization whether or not they have children. This important service within the community has a huge impact on not only the youth they are directly serving, but on the parents they working with. There are so many opportunities for us to use the gifts and talents we have been given.

No matter what work we do, we remember our purpose. Our purpose is not to attain status or titles in society so that others see us as "important" or "successful." Our purpose is not to do good works in order to earn our way to heaven. Our purpose in life is not even to satisfy ourselves and our desires. Rick Warren, author of *A Purpose Driven Life*, says that we were "put on earth to make a contribution" (Warren, pg. 227). Our purpose is to share the Word of God with others through our talents and gifts and be humble in so doing so that others may want what we have. We are to empower others by fulfilling our purpose as stated in Ephesians 2:10: "For we are God's workmanship, created in Christ Jesus to do good works, which God prepared in advance for us to do."

Determining the Impact

You may feel called to leave all of your earthly possessions behind and embark on mission work in a remote village in Africa. Your spouse may or may not be enthusiastic about sharing this vision. As you have made a *commitment* to each other, you need to find the common ground of how you see fulfilling your purpose while keeping your family intact.

You may feel called to be your child's Little League coach, Cub Scout leader, and Sunday school teacher. Each of these on its own is noble service. But how much time does the preparation and service take away from your family and your spouse? Herein lies the balancing act and compromise that two people must make when determining how to fulfill their purpose. Sacrifices may need to be made as one spouse goes back to school or one decides to quit their job and stay home with children and get involved in their activities. Once we establish our purpose, we can figure out our action plan in order to make our purpose a reality. Having a spouse to consider when determining the impact of our action plan may mean that it might not move as quickly as we think it should.

Instead of quitting a job altogether, we may have to take night school classes over the period of a few years to earn the degree. This may mean finding a way to work from home in order to stay home with the children. Each couple must decide the best way for each spouse to fulfill his or her purpose in life. It may also mean taking turns in order for both spouses to be able to do what they were meant to do.

We must go back to being selfless when determining the impact that our work has on our spouse while at the same time remaining focused and steadfast in our purpose. If we are working toward what we were meant to do with a pure heart and pure intentions, our spouse will recognize our goal and meet us in the middle as he strives to be selfless as well. How empowering two selfless people can be when determining the greatest impact they can have in this world!

Establishing a Support Structure

You know how draining your work can be. There are days when I come home so mentally, physically, and emotionally exhausted that I wonder if what I'm doing is worth it. These are the days that Steve realizes I need a little time and a little extra tender loving care. He asks the boys to pitch in around the house more than normal and to understand that I may have had a rough day. His support makes it easier for me to ease out of the day and back into the role of wife

Amy Bindas

and mother with renewed vigor and commitment to doing my best.

If we do not understand what our spouse may be going through, it may breed resentment or feelings of not being appreciated for the work we do outside of the home. Once again, we need to be selfless in order to foster the marriage and the home. Believe me, when both spouses have had difficult days, it isn't easy to set them aside, but communicating with each other allows us to negotiate those rough waters.

Before realizing the importance of this support, Steve and I would come home from very different days and have an "every man for himself" attitude. If one of us had a rough day, we didn't talk about it or share the details nearly enough as we just wanted to get past it. This led to the withholding of feelings and thus resentment. It was almost a competition to see who could work through their mood the fastest in order to feel human again. This lack of supporting each other drove us further and further away from finding the strength to go into the world another day to serve others.

I have learned to give Steve information about my day along the way. Small bits through e-mail and text are vital for him to know what I've faced when we come back together. He will share thoughts and feelings about what he is going through as well so that we can feel connected, even as we go through very different experiences on a daily basis.

This goes back to the vital daily *communication* checkpoints. When we finally get that time to talk, we have a frame of reference of the struggles as well as the celebrations we have had. This helps us better know how to approach each other and then how to support each other. In the end, this helps us process, relax, and renew so that we can get up the next day and continue serving with the right heart and the right spirit toward our individual missions.

This is also the reason that our marriage needs to be Christ-centered. Coming back into our home for rejuvenation from the world that seeks to destroy us is crucial. Even though I crave support from my spouse, I must also remember that my ultimate support comes from God. He tells me to give my burdens to Him because my spouse, as well-intentioned as he is, may not always offer that opportunity. Jesus must become my first source of comfort, my first source of strength, and my first source of support if I am to carry out my purpose in the community. As Psalm 68:19 reminds us, "Praise be to the Lord, To God our Savior, who daily bears our burdens." Jesus also implores us in Matthew 11:28, "Come to me, all you who are weary and burdened, and I will give your rest."

Remember, Paul said it is better for us to be single as there is no distraction then to our true purpose here on earth. But if we "cannot control" ourselves, it is much better to be married. The Laffoons say it this way: "Decide your master first...second, decide your mission...last, decide your mate" (Laffoon, pg. 120). What does this mean? We still have a mission and a purpose on earth—to live out and spread the Word of God—and we need to determine how best each one of us can do that. Then we need to understand how our spouse sees his mission and how we can support him. In the end, this mutual support is critical in living out our purposes.

Chapter 7
Reflection Activity:
Supporting Your Spouse in
Serving Your Community

This activity may require deep personal reflection. The process may lead you to need time alone, or it may lead you to realize you need to talk through some thoughts with someone else. This process cannot be rushed as you are considering your true life's mission. When you are comfortable with that, you need to share it with your spouse. Your spouse is one that knows many things about you and can help you in this process. But he or she will need to do this selflessly, focusing on your mission and not how it will impact your current reality.

1. We all have different gifts and talents, and when we are using these talents to the glory of God, we are at our highest point of being fulfilled in our

purpose. Write down what your individual gifts and talents are.

2. List some ways you can live out God's word through your gifts and talents.

3. Consider how pursuing your purpose will impact your family. Write down any thoughts of impact.

4. Consider this: can your spouse support you in your goals? Write down any ideas.

5. Take turns sharing your insights.

6. Prayer:

Father, You have provided a spouse for us to strengthen and support us. Let us have confidence not only in our marriages but in our abilities that we may go into the world and do Your work. In doing Your work, we are truly living out our purpose. Thank You for the individual gifts and talents You have given us to make this work possible. In Jesus's name we pray, amen.

Conclusion:
Charting Your Course

Folly delights a man who lacks judgment, but a man of understanding keeps a straight course.

—Proverbs 15:21

God is immense enough to be in all places at one time. He can oversee all of us simultaneously and knows our thoughts as His own. It is like He is looking down over us on our journey, yearning for us to follow the right path, and blessing us when we do, but not forgetting about us if we don't. He has charted a course for us on our sailing journey, and it's up to us whether or not to follow it. Regardless of our strong will one way or the other, like a father that loves and is committed to his children, He is still always there looking over us.

In the end, it's our choice. Everything is our choice—to follow God's *command*, to *commit* to our spouse, to *communicate* effectively and sincerely, to prioritize *couple time*, to keep *Christ at the center* of our marriage, to make wise decisions about the blessings of our *currency*, and to support our spouse and to use our own skills and talents productively within the *community* for God's purpose.

God didn't promise that our journey would be easy. I am not a sailor, but I have observed that sailing looks like a lot of work. Reading the maps, charting the course, navigating through the rough waters safely, securing the vessel, and interpreting the instruments simultaneously does not look like an easy job. As you know, neither is navigating marriage on a daily basis. As we practice and learn from our mistakes, we get better at it, and it is easier to get it right. God wants us to have this in mind because it can be the most blessed and fulfilling journey of our lives.

Look around at other people's marriages, especially those that are Christian. You will see some that are getting it right and some aren't. What message is that sending to those within the church as well as to those on the outside looking in? We must be role models in practicing the skills that will make our marriages fun and fulfilling. We must support our friends and neighbors who need help and direction. If this is sounding like a desperate plea, that's because it is.

The roots of a healthy society are healthy families, and the foundation of a healthy family is a healthy marriage. We have an obligation to God, who gave us the gift of marriage along with instructions on how to get it right, to study those instructions and know them well. As I mentioned earlier, there are many people in our world today who want to see the "institution" of marriage fail so that their social constructs rise as better alternatives. You can have the marriage you've always dreamed about, and you can help others attain that goal as well.

As we sail the seven *C*s of marriage, we need to rely on the Word of God to chart our course and for His wisdom to guide our journey. As we build our marriages to be strong ships setting sail on our lifelong journey together, we remember that we can't set a straight course or weather strong winds and waves without God. He provides our itinerary, our compass, and our hope in the storms. Most importantly, He provides our anchor. He is our anchor in wind, rain, storms, and general times of trouble. He promises that with Him we will not wander off course. With Him we will not capsize. With Him we will not drift.

May your journey be one of faith, hope, and love, but may it be anchored in the greatest of these—love!

Appendix A

COVENANT PLEDGE

God created you as a unique individual. I committed to become your husband/wife because…

As we grow in our marriage, I would like to renew my commitment to you at this time because…

You are the one I will sacrifice my own needs for. You are the one I will try to serve to the best of my ability, and you are the one who completes me as one flesh.

_____   _____
Signature   Date

Bibliography

Chapman, Gary. *Covenant Marriage*. Broadman and Holman, 2003.

Chapman, Gary. *The Five Love Languages*. Northfield Publishing, 2004.

Farrel, Bill and Farrel, Pam, *Men Are Like Waffles–Women Are Like Spaghetti*,

Gungor, Mark. Laugh Your Way to a Better Marriage. www.laughyourway.com, 2009.

Laffoon, Jay and Laura Laffoon. *The Spark*. Baker Publishing Group, 2008.

Money Magazine. http://money.cnn.com.

Palmer, Bethany and Scott Palmer. *First Comes Love, Then Comes Money*.

Todorova, Aleksandra. "The Six Financial Mistakes Couples Make." *Family Money*, (June 2008).

Warren, Rick. *A Purpose Driven Life*. Zondervan, 2002.

White Smith, Debra. *Romancing Your Husband*. Harvest House, 2002.